An Afternoon's Dictation

Inclusive Revelation for the 21st Century

Steven Greenebaum

Copyeditor: Betty Lou Leaver
Cover design: James B. Tinney
Book layout: Opeyemi Ikuborije

ISBN: 978-1-957354-24-8

LCCN: 2022952096

CONTENTS

Part Four: The Call to Justice

Part Five: The Call to Community

Part Six: Some Conundrums Regarding the Divine

INTRODUCTION

These are hugely difficult times. When I began this book, COVID was loose and taking lives across the country and around the world as wars were raging and murdering so many innocents. Now, as wars continue, there are new diseases raging while many struggle to learn to live with "long COVID." All this as people are at long last recognizing that the environment is in crisis yet continue to argue vehemently over what if anything to do about it. In the United States and much of what has been called the "free world," the very nature of freedom itself is the topic of vehement and often virulent argument. The future of the Earth is in question. More personally, and for me of equal importance, the quality of life we are leaving for posterity is also in question. Even if, as I fervently hope, humanity at last rises to the occasion and begins to work in earnest to save itself and the planet, there are some dark times ahead—very dark times.

In the face of this darkness, why write a book? Particularly with my health so "iffy," why spend what energy remains to me writing? For me, the answer is hope. Yet, hope without action becomes merely a dream that disappears with the morning. So, I write.

I deeply believe that if we are to find our way out of the darkness we will need to come together. We will need to find and cleave to what can unite us. We will need, if you will, a positive, hopeful, action-based spiritual renewal.

To be clear, this book cannot be and is in no way intended to provide "the answer." My hope is that it may help us to navigate our journey through the darkness to find and renew our spiritual selves. How? Reasonable question! In this book, I want to share fully what was shared with me some twenty years ago at a time when I had lost all sense of optimism and was sinking into a personal abyss of darkness. The why of the abyss may be found in my spiritual memoir, *"One Family: Indivisible."* In brief, for several months in 1999, in the privacy of my home, I angrily demanded, several times every day, frequently out loud and sometimes in my mind, "God, you're there? I want five minutes, and I want answers!"

Of course, it is one thing to demand answers but quite another to actually get them! After months of pleading for answers to the great questions of my life, an inner voice that I knew wasn't mine told me to get some paper and a pen and write. Ok, then! I got paper and, well, took dictation. Three pages of it.

The honest truth of it is that having received the revelations I'd so angrily demanded, I had no idea what to do with them. I then pondered, indeed studied and lived with these revelations, for roughly ten years before things at last gelled. Parts of the dictation made immediate sense. Yet other parts became clear only after a *lot* of study.

These revelations changed my life. In the end, not only did I feel I understood what had been revealed to me, but I was also launched upon the path of Interfaith that I have walked ever since. What was revealed to me that day has not only given me purpose and direction but also hope—hope for myself, and for humanity.

Out of those years of studying the revelations I'd been gifted, three books slowly emerged. My first book, *The Interfaith Alternative*, was derived directly from my study of the revelations, which had not only set me on the path of respecting the diversity of our spiritual traditions but also caused me to found the Living Interfaith church. The second book, *Practical Interfaith*, came two years later and in answer to those who had said, "Interfaith sounds beautiful, but is it practical?" It was based on what I had learned in the day-to-day world about actually starting an Interfaith congregation. Five years later came my third book, *One Family: Indivisible*. It was a personal sharing, warts and all, of my spiritual life from childhood to the present, including the receipt of the revelations and how I came to embrace the whole of the human family as my own.

One might reasonably ask, "Why wait to share the revelations until the third book?" This decision was based on life experience. Rightly or wrongly, I felt that there was so much controversy over the question of God (Is there a God or isn't there; and if there is, what is the nature of God?) that I believed if I started with the revelations, too many people would be distracted by asking, was it from God or not? I believed then, as I believe now, that the call of Interfaith is a call to all of us—ALL of us. It calls to us whether we embrace God or not and regardless of how we relate to God, if indeed we believe.

So, I included the revelations in *One Family: Indivisible* and did so pretty much without comment. At the time, it felt wrong to be adding any interpretations. This feeling was based on a private fear. I feared being seen as some kind of prophet. Good flaming grief, all I am and ever will be is the *very* human and imperfect me. The last thing I wanted was a discussion about me to get in the way of the call to Interfaith even as I felt obligated to share the dictation. Happily, I am now thoroughly convinced that no one is *ever* going to confuse me with a prophet, nor should they. Ever! But as I talked to and heard from people who'd read the book, I came to realize that sharing the revelations without comment had left the work unfinished. So here, in what will be my final book, I want not only to share the dictation again but also what I made of it. After twenty years of pondering and working with it, what has been revealed?

As I hope will be clear, I am in no way attempting to provide the last word on the revelations. My thoughts are *not* intended to end discussion. What I hope is that they can be a beginning. I will share what was dictated to me and what, after long hours and years of living with it, I believe it communicates: a message of hope, and a guide for those of us who want to live meaningful lives. I also want to share what I made of that message and why.

Still, that sharing is only my take. I can only write about what I know. So, among other things, it's important to acknowledge that I write from a Western perspective. I am also aware that I write from a Jewish perspective, albeit as part of the Reform movement. Orthodox Jews, not to mention folks from spiritual traditions other than Judaism, will, I feel sure, read and adapt what's here to their own experiences and needs. Yes, I believe we are all one family.

But let's be honest, our family has been separated a very long time.

In addition, as I delved further and further into our diverse spiritual traditions and their histories, it became ever clearer that the enlightenment I'd received had been received by so very many before me. Yes, the wording may be different. I'm a Western English speaker, living at that moment at the cusp of the 21st century, but the essence was the same. So, please do expect some *déjà vu* as you read. The message isn't new. We've heard it again and again across the centuries. My guess is that we will keep hearing it over and over until we stop preaching about it and actually act—integrating it into our lives as a family.

In the appendices, I share two gently different versions of the dictation I received. The first is a recounting of the revelations as I wrote them down. The second is a reorganization, and only that, of the order of the revelations into the groupings that occurred to me after I'd lived with them for well over ten years. These are the groupings that make up the six sections of the book. For clarity, each chapter will contain the relevant revelations in a large font.

As *An Afternoon's Dictation* is published, however deep the hole in which we find ourselves, we face a basic truth. We can accept living in that deep hole or not. And if we reject living in this emotional and spiritual hole, we are going to need each other to climb out. However difficult and long that climb, I believe we owe the effort to our children and to children yet to come. And as we make that climb, may we free our souls of the fear of "them" that has so crippled our efforts to this moment.

I particularly want to include in our effort to climb out of that darkness, those of my human family who question all spiritual paths, and most particularly any who feel excluded as "other" by people who cleave to a particular path and a particular definition of the divine. We are in this together, all of us. Let us exclude none of good will and join hands as we come together to free ourselves from the spiritual abyss.

We must hang on to hope and each other—and then work together to make that hope real. We are one family. If we will embrace that and work together, we may just come through this.

Last, I want to hold high two important books that have been and remain hugely helpful. There are indeed many important and wonderful books out there. I want to point out two books on the scriptures of our world's spiritual traditions that I've found especially valuable. *One Heart: Universal Wisdom from the World's Scriptures* (Marlowe & Company) and *World Scripture: A Comparative Anthology of Sacred Text"* (Paragon House). I am grateful for both books, and the reader should know that as I sought examples from differing scriptures, I particularly consulted these two books and have used them as a source for quotes throughout the book. A heartfelt THANK YOU to Andrew Wilson, who edited *World Scripture*, and Bonnie Louise Kuchler, who edited *One Heart*. I would strongly recommend both books to anyone seeking to delve even more deeply into our diverse and profound scriptures.

AN AFTERNOON'S DICTATION

PART ONE:
The Call to Interfaith

CHAPTER ONE

In 1999, I'd reached the end of my tether. Over the years, there had been one crushing event after another. The woman I'd intended to spend my life with, who had intended to spend her life with me, had been killed in a senseless traffic accident. My mother, who had lived her life fettered by the chains of patriarchy, had at last broken free and blossomed, recognizing her own self-worth, only to be struck down by cancer after just a few short years of truly enjoying life. And then my father, with whom I'd had major disagreements but whom I loved and honored as my father, had died a humiliating death, plagued by dementia.

These were just the tips of the iceberg. I was one angry human. In the privacy of my house, I kept saying, sometimes out loud and sometimes in my mind, "God, you're there? Really? I want five minutes, and I want some answers." Then, after several months of expressing my anger, I got answers--well over five minutes' worth. I took three pages of dictation--revelation, if you will, and not only about life and death.

What set me on my heels was that I had gotten answers to so much more than I had been asking about. Indeed, the tragedies that so oppressed my mind didn't even come up until mid-way through the dictation. What came first were answers to huge questions that had been echoing somewhere in the corners of my brain for years but that I'd never actually put into words.

Living an Interfaith life is today so completely who I am that it is sobering to realize that I'd reached the age of 50 without ever seriously thinking about it. It wasn't foremost on my mind. Not even close. It was not a part of my day-to-day life. It wasn't something I'd spent time pondering. And frankly, while I dutifully wrote down the revelations as they were given to me, my immediate interest was riveted on what came roughly halfway through, most particularly two revelations. I'll deal with them and their broader meaning more fully in the next section, but for now, they threw me both a mental and spiritual life preserver.

You cannot live forever, but you can be with Me forever. Time is your measure, not Mine.

At this point in my life, I didn't have any sort of handle on who or what God was or might be. But here was the comforting assertion that the woman I'd loved, whose life had been cut so horrifically short by a flaming traffic accident, would forever be with God, whoever or whatever God was. The same for my mom, and even my imperfect father. This gave me the chance to breathe again. But what about *how* they died?

The mind is not the soul. Nor is the body. Sometimes, the mind decays or the body writhes with pain before the soul has left it. That is indeed a tragedy. Weep, but do not despair.

This was like God throwing comforting arms around me. My father had tried hard to instill in me his belief that "real men" don't cry. Now, with "Weep, but do not despair," I had permission to acknowledge my tears. God was telling me that horrible things do indeed happen. Tragedy happens. Acknowledge that. Accept that. It is terrible. Weep, yes, weep, but do not despair. You still live. There are things you can do. You have a life. LIVE IT! Wow!

That helped. It helped a great deal. Still, it wasn't lost on me that while these were the pressing issues in my life at this moment, they weren't where the dictation started. Clearly, they were important enough to me that the call of the sacred indeed answered them; but they didn't come first. They didn't come up until midway through the revelations. I had received comfort and reassurance, but clearly there was more to this. I was also supposed to do something. Me? I was supposed to do something? Good grief! What??

A few months later, after I'd recovered from the initial shock of what had been given to me, I scooped up the dictation and travelled south to Oregon to visit my longtime friend and now retired Methodist minister, Rev. Wes Yamaka. I showed him the dictation I'd received.

"Am I nuts?" I asked him.

"No," he told me. "You're not nuts." Then he handed the revelations back to me.

"So, what are you going to do with this?" he asked.

"I don't know," I replied.

"Do you think you should sit on it?"

"No."

"So, how do you intend to share it?" When I just looked at him, Wes added, "Tell you what. Once you've written the book, if you feel like it, I'd love to read it."

Yikes! Ok, then, that clarified things. I had a lot to think about. First and foremost, it seemed to me, I really did have to think about this. I had to live with the revelations, ponder them, and then try to come to grips with this dictation I'd been handed. I was well aware that I couldn't "do" anything until I had grappled with and better understood what it was I'd been given. Thus began what ended up being about ten years of pondering and groping with what had been revealed to me. And the first question to grapple with was why was "Religion is but a language for speaking to Me" the first revelation? Why was this number one?

I'd been a Jew all my life, still was, and had no interest in leaving Judaism. That said, I'd met some wonderful Christians; and while my immediate knowledge at that point in my life was only about Judaism and Christianity, I knew that there were a multitude of other religions. I'd studied ancient history and not only knew of but deeply respected the ancient Greeks. They'd believed in a whole pantheon of gods, led by Zeus. Christianity and Judaism, while firmly parting company over the divinity of Jesus, were at least related, particularly in their belief in one God. Yet the Greeks were brilliant thinkers. What had happened? I also knew of Buddhism and Islam (though at that time, little more than that they existed and a lot of humanity followed those spiritual teachings). How could this be? So many differing religions. If there is only one "right" answer, how could this possibly be?

And now, with the dictation, my first revelation did not concern what angered me. Instead, it answered this deeply spiritual question that had been quietly nagging at me for decades.

Religion is but a language for speaking to Me. Think ye that arbol is better than tree? Was Old English a "false language" because you now speak modern English?

Religion is a language? At first, that didn't make sense. And yet, after I sat with it and pondered it, it did make sense. It made a lot of sense. No, the Spanish word *arbol* isn't a better or worse word than the English word *tree*. No, Old English wasn't a false language, just as the beliefs of the ancient Greeks weren't a false religion. Humanity changes. Cultures change. Language changes. Different doesn't mean better or worse. Now that I grasped it, this became for me an important, indeed life-altering, revelation.

The door to this revelation began to open wide as I reacted to catastrophic events that occurred about two years after the dictation. It was September 11, 2001. It wasn't solely the horrific events of September 11 but also people's reaction to them that made clear to me the need for a world where we didn't kill each other over our differing religious beliefs. I grew up right after the Holocaust/Shoah. As a kid, it took me a while to realize that it wasn't Christianity that caused the extermination of over six million Jews. It was the belief in the absolute rightness and supremacy of Christianity that allowed some fanatics to accept that killing Jews was somehow "holy." After September 11, as so many turned to a blind hatred of Islam, I didn't know a lot about the religion. Yet, I did know enough to understand that it wasn't Islam that caused 9-11. It was belief in the absolute rightness and supremacy of Islam that allowed some fanatics to accept the idea that blowing people up in the name of Allah was somehow "holy."

This brought home to me why "religion is a language" was first on the list of revelations. 9-11 and people's reaction to it also helped me to realize that I needed to dig deeper into things , a *lot* deeper. I needed not just to ponder this, I needed to study it. I needed to study other religions. Okay, that's a lot of study and a lot of books!

My study began, but certainly did not end, with *Rescuing the Bible from Fundamentalism* by Bishop John Shelby Spong. I then read book after book. Still, after more than two years of reading I realized I needed to dig into this even more deeply. To do that, I needed structure. Go back to school? Really? Ok, where? A Jew speaking only to Jews didn't seem to work for me. But what to do? At this moment, I was the choir director at a Unitarian Universalist fellowship. Was that the answer? In 2004, I began exploring the possibility of becoming a Unitarian Universalist minister. Me? A minister? Me???

I realized I needed to study theology far more thoroughly than I possibly could by staying at home and reading. So, I applied to Seattle University's School of Theology and Ministry and started my studies there the summer of 2005. I received a Master's in Pastoral Studies in 2007 (for more details and context, please see my spiritual memoir, *One Family: Indivisible*).

By then, I'd come to realize that my calling wasn't Unitarian Universalism. My calling was Interfaith. And central to that calling were the revelations I'd lived with and pondered now for eight years and counting. And at the core of that Interfaith calling was this first and deeply foundational revelation.

CHAPTER TWO

"Religion is but a language for speaking to Me." It's hard to overstate how crucial this revelation was.

In the 50 years of my life that preceded the revelation, that thought had never once occurred to me, now that it was laid in in my lap it made perfect sense. It made sense and answered a bucket-full of questions. The first and most pressing question it answered for me was this: if there were indeed one and only one "right" answer to the question of God and how to relate to God, why didn't humanity know what that answer was? After thousands upon thousands of years, why were there so many differing answers?

The ancient Greeks were no dummies. They'd gifted us Sophocles, Socrates, Aristotle, Plato, and so many other brilliant thinkers. If the truth of it is that there is only one God, why did the Greeks worship twelve? The ancient Hebrews embraced one God, as did Christianity, but Christians quickly divided God into three very different aspects (Father, Son, Holy Spirit). So, which was it, one God or a God with three very different personas? And then there was Buddhism. The Buddha, as best as I understood him in 1999, embraced the sacred but not God. I didn't really know much at all about Islam at that time, but I did understand this was yet another way of approaching God. And there were the Native Americans and indigenous peoples around the world. I had a Masters in mythology. I knew of the diversity and, yes, profundity of our many myths. So again, if there were truly one and only one answer, why were there so many different spiritual traditions? I could not, and do not, subscribe to the idea that God is incompetent. Yet, if God were not incompetent, then what gives? Could it be that there *is* no one right answer?

The idea that one group of people, be they Hebrews, Christians, Muslims, Buddhists, or any other group, somehow "got it right" and everyone else was wrong seemed an incredibly arrogant way of seeing our religious differences. Earlier in my life, I'd quit my job as High Holy Days choir director at a temple because the cantor there kept insisting that Judaism was the one right religion. I felt deeply that Judaism was "an answer" and a good answer for me. That said, to leap to the conclusion that because it was good for me it was the one right answer for everyone seemed hugely arrogant. Still, I had no real answer as to why there could be so many good and righteous spiritual traditions. Now, "Religion is but a language for speaking to Me" made things crystal clear. It was a spiritual awakening, the dawning of what would become my new life. I had briefly studied comparative linguistics and more deeply studied comparative mythology. It now became clear that the two were far more closely linked than I had thought.

As I wrote in my first book on Interfaith (for a fuller context, see *The Interfaith Alternative*. New Society Publishers, 2012, especially pages 85-88.), "A language is neither good nor evil. A language is neither true nor false. A language can neither save nor damn you. A work of incredible beauty and profound significance can be written in any language and indeed has been. The fact that a profound book has been written in Russian, Chinese, Latin, or Swahili does not lessen its value. It simply needs to be translated into words we can relate to and understand. It *needs to be translated into words we can relate to and understand.* Old English was not a "false language." But we no longer speak it, and so Old English too must be translated."

Does this mean our spiritual traditions aren't important? No! I believe our traditions are deeply important. Try communicating with someone without using language. Indeed, try thinking about anything, let alone sacred matters, without using language. We *need* language. What it *does* mean is that like all of humanity's languages, past and present, our sacred language will vary from era to era and culture to culture.

It came to me that seeing our religions and spiritual traditions as crucially important languages for speaking to and about the sacred but not structured repositories of the one right way of approaching it allows us to find answers to questions that have been around since humanity first began thinking about them.

First, and perhaps foremost, seeing our spiritual pathways as languages allows us to answer the question: "If there is only one right spiritual pathway, why after all these centuries haven't we found it?" Some Christians may say that they have the one right answer. Some Jews may disagree and say *they* have the one right answer. Some Muslims, Buddhist, Hindi, Jain, and so many others may think they have the one right answer. Yet the truth of it is most of humanity has never, *not once,* ever adhered to a belief in the correctness of any one single path. Not once! There may indeed be millions of Christians, but there are also millions of Buddhists, Baha'i, Muslims, and so many others.

Yet if our spiritual traditions are languages for dealing with how we see and speak about the sacred, then much that has been blurry comes into focus. Differing languages develop differently, depending not only on culture but also on the geography of where the speakers live. As one example, it has been reported the Inuit (Eskimo) have scores of gradations for words meaning snow, but the English speaker has far fewer. Does that make the Inuit "right"? No. Does it make the English speaker "right"? Again, no. How one describes and deals with snow depends on where you live. If I live where there is snow on the ground every day and every night and indeed build my lodging from snow (as in an igloo), how I relate to snow will be very different from someone who only sees and interacts with snow in the winter, if then. It doesn't make one person "right" and the other a heretic.

Our religions and diverse spiritual traditions aren't, then, unchangeable. Nor should we expect them to be. They are living, breathing languages for talking to and about the sacred. Crucial, yes! Crucial spiritual languages.

The deal was closed, if you will, with the revelation that followed.

Many have spoken for Me. They were righteous, and they did carry My words. But I am not human, and you are not God. Language can be a barrier between us as well as yourselves that can be all but impossible to breach. Seek truth in the commonality of religions—which are but the languages of speaking to Me. Worship not the grammar.

This one I had to ponder a bit, but as I did, it made such sense! If God, Spirit, Cosmic Conscience, or whatever we choose to call it, reaches out to us, that outreach has to be in a language we can understand or it will make no sense. If, as example, we receive an *absolute truth* in the revelation, "Mobli abuti, dicot bavariun, picicumaticus landri, biuntic jovand," what can we do with it? Nothing. No matter how true, there is nothing we can do. The simple fact is, we can only understand revelation in terms of the language we know (see Appendix C, "Shavuot Sermon"). And our languages differ. Not only is English different from French, Spanish, and so many other languages, but the English in the United States differs from that in Great Britain, Australia, and other English-speaking countries. Indeed, there are differences in English across the United States. If our languages are different, how we hear revelations of the sacred will be different. That's why the revelatory guidance: "Seek truth in the commonality of religions" became a driving force in my life.

Wow! Don't seek the truth of the one "right" religion. Seek truth in the commonality of religions. That was going to take work. Indeed, it took years, and much study, but this revelation is what brought me to embrace Interfaith and specifically Interfaith as a faith. "Seek truth in the commonality of religions." If we will embrace that, we are freed from so much. That said, being shown an open door is meaningless unless we are willing to walk through it. In Chapter 4, we'll make that attempt! Yes, it took time—years of study. And the first thing I had to grapple with was "worship not the grammar."

Grammar is essential. No language will make sense without the rules of grammar that organize it. Yet every language has different rules, a different grammar. Should an adjective go before or after the noun? Obvious? No. In English, we say it's a beautiful house. In Spanish, however, it's a house beautiful. In German, the verbs can show up in places they never would in English, but is one right and the others wrong? No! As crucially important as grammar is in organizing each of our languages, there can be no value judgement as to which grammar is "right." So, religious grammar? Worship not the grammar. What would that mean?

For one thing, it would mean letting go of the sense of "rightness" of our differing rituals. Rituals may perhaps best be thought a part of the grammar that helps us to order our spiritual traditions. To be clear, our rituals can be crucial, as crucial as grammar is to making sense of a language. It's when we chisel our rituals into stone, righteous and unchangeable, that we lose our way.

I'm a Jew, born in the United States. My native language is English. Should my prayers be in Hebrew or English (or Aramaic)? It's a question of grammar. If I'm Catholic, should my prayers be in my native language or Latin? Again, grammar. Should my head be covered when I pray? Grammar. Is there a particular direction in which I should pray (like Muslims face Mecca), and should I be on my knees or prostrate? More grammar. Again, grammar is important. When I was the choir director at a Reconstructionist Jewish temple, I needed to be able to understand Hebrew to successfully lead the choir. I needed to learn to read Hebrew because as a Jew in the Reform movement, while reciting prayers in Hebrew was a part of the tradition, actually learning Hebrew wasn't; it was an encouraged option, not a requirement. I could be, and indeed was, confirmed as a member of our Reform congregation without what is called a Bar Mitzvah. That's the Reform movement. For Reconstructionists, however, Hebrew was essential. Was one right and the other wrong? I would say no. It was a difference of religious grammar. And now it was clear: "Worship not the grammar."

Not that I was in any way off the hook. "Seek truth in the commonality of religions." Okay then, if I were truly going to seek truth, I needed to study religions, a lot of religions. More than that, I needed to stop judging the grammar of other spiritual traditions. What I was charged with was *not* to be bothered by our differences, but to seek truth by seeking what our diverse religions held in common. For me, that meant nearly a decade of study.

Last, and before we leave the subject, there's the rather crucial question of who is this "Me" we keep talking about? "Religion is but a language for speaking to Me." Who is this "Me"?

Many would say God, but then, in all honesty, they would likely then argue over how to define "God." Who or what is God? Is God a he? Or a she? Others would say there is no God, but there is a moral force in the universe, and then argue over the nature of that moral force. Still others would embrace the idea that there is a sacred "something" that we should cleave to, without placing any name on it. Then, being the rather arrogant humans that we are, we would argue about it, often passionately, sometimes violently. Who's right? If our religions and spiritual traditions are languages for speaking to and about the sacred—languages that keep changing over time and circumstance—then, as there is no one "right" language, there is no one "right" answer to how we speak to and about the sacred.

As for me, I embrace Thomas Huxley's approach. I'm agnostic. The cold hard fact of the matter is: I don't know. My life-experience has led me to believe that there is indeed a moral force in the universe that I personally relate to as Cosmic Conscience. I call that Cosmic Conscience God but have no interest in arguing about it. I believe in God, but I'm also agnostic. I realize that my beliefs are not knowledge.

The critical truth of it is that most, if not all, of us want to be able to speak to and about the sacred, however we choose to define it. This is fundamental to our spiritual lives. Our religions are then hugely important and not to be belittled. Our religions give us the language to grapple with this so very important part of our lives. That these languages have developed over time and developed differently not only over time but also from culture to culture in no way diminishes them.

So, ok, fine. Religions are languages to speak to and about the sacred. What do we do about it? Which brings us to one of the holiest of expressions of our religious languages: scripture.

CHAPTER THREE

Scripture has long fascinated me. Growing up Jewish, my first experience with scripture was, of course, Hebrew scripture. Most particularly, I was introduced to and schooled in the first five books of Hebrew scripture, what we call Torah. Torah is considered particularly sacred and important. And the study of Torah is considered a life-long task. As Rabbi Tarfon put it some 2,000 years ago, we can never finish our study, but that does not mean we can or should avoid it ("Pirke Avot" 2:16).

That approach to scripture calls to me. Consider what it means that we are not called to memorize our sacred writings. Nor are we called to read scripture once or twice, or even three times and then put it away. We are called to study it. And as we won't be studying scripture alone, it means that we will discuss it and from time to time even argue about it, though amiably one hopes. And we are called to keep revisiting it. The implication, for me, is that scripture is to be considered a living, breathing document, not a text frozen in time. How we look at scripture and interpret it will, then, change, not only over the millennia of human history, but also over our own lifetimes as our life-experiences change (in the Appendix, I share a recent example, a new revelation that resulted in a reexamination and then reinterpretation of the 23rd Psalm).

There is as well an intriguing question of what's to be done when scripture flat out contradicts itself? Say what? The first contradiction that leapt out at me as a youth, and indeed seemed to grab me by my lapels and say "Look!" was in the very first book of Torah: Genesis. According to Genesis 1:27, on the *sixth* day, God created male and female, both in God's own image and at the same time. But then, according to Genesis 2:7-23, it's *after* the *seventh* day that God created the first human. Adam and only Adam was created from the dust of the ground. God then breathed life into him. Only after creating the Garden of Eden did God think that Adam shouldn't be alone. So God created ... not the first woman, but the beasts of the field and the fowl of the air. It was then, only then, when this still wasn't enough, that God, seemingly as an afterthought, created Eve—not from the dust of the ground and by breathing life into her as Adam was created but by causing Adam to go to sleep and taking one of his ribs.

What infuriated me, even as a youth, was that it was this second story that everyone knew and quoted. It was as if the first account didn't exist! That there were two stories was certainly intriguing, but for some reason, that didn't bother me as much. It seemed another good reason to remember to study Torah, not merely glance at it and never look back, but that we so completely adopted the story that made Eve's creation an afterthought was one more reminder of the cancer of patriarchy that I believed so plagued Judaism (patriarchy has been a life-long "hot button" issue for me – for context, see *One Family: Indivisible*).

Having two diametrically opposed stories of human creation also taught me that however much scripture might begin as the word of God, we have received that word through imperfect human hands. What I took from my studies was that scripture could not and did not provide unmitigated, unchangeable truth. This, it seemed to me, was what Rabbi Tarfon (and so many others) had been talking about. Study Torah, and keep studying it. And don't just mindlessly study: think about it!

Another important reason for studying Torah came as I contemplated two other crucial passages. The first was in Genesis (18:20-33). God is angry at the sins of the people of Sodom and Gomorrah and plans to obliterate them. Yet, Abraham doesn't say, "Yes, Lord. Whatever you say, Lord. I am your servant, Lord. I will do whatever you tell me to do." No. Instead of blind obedience, Abraham argues that it would be wrong to destroy everyone in the cities if there might be good people as well. Abraham starts with 50, and once God agrees to spare the cities if there are 50 righteous people, Abraham keeps arguing until the number gets down to ten. Now, there aren't ten, and God destroys the cities. But Abraham arguing with God about justice? Wow! That's indeed a life-lesson!

The clincher came in Exodus (32:7-15). God and Moses are having a nice chat atop Mount Sinai, where, among other things, Moses receives the Decalogue (the Ten Commandments), but below them, hearing nothing from Moses or God, the Children of Israel grow restless and fashion a golden calf to worship. They are ready to forget God and worship a golden calf! God loses it and is ready to wipe the Children of Israel off the face of the Earth—each and every one of them! But like Abraham before him, Moses doesn't say "Yes, Lord. Whatever you say, Lord." Instead, Moses argues that to lash out in anger and obliterate a people would be wrong. It would not be just. Moses has the courage, perhaps even the audacity, to tell God to repent. Again, that's Moses telling God to repent! And God does. Again, wow!

What to make of this? This is fundamental stuff, coming from the Torah, the most sacred text of Jewish scripture. Do I personally believe that Abraham and Moses actually got God to put aside irrational anger and a thirst for violence? No, I don't. But there it is, in scripture! If our scriptures are the inerrant, immovable Word of God, it makes no sense, but if our scriptures are not a never-changing rulebook and instead are a very human attempt to interpret the Word of God, to be studied, pondered, discussed, and, from time to time, even argued about, then it makes perfect sense.

What I took from these passages in Genesis and Exodus is a significantly important lesson in not blindly following authority. I don't believe in a God who loses it one moment, only to be saved from destructive anger by human interaction. What I see and am guided by is a lesson from God that *no* call to injustice should be obeyed, regardless of where it comes from, even if we think it comes from God. God is teaching us (as well as Abraham and Moses) that it is justice that counts. I believe in a cosmic call to justice that was glad, even relieved, that Abraham and Moses rose to take the "bait" and argued. Obey the call of justice! That is an immensely important lesson. I fear it is a lesson that humanity continues to struggle with to this very day.

"Now wait!" you may well say. At least, I hope you will. This is just your interpretation; it's just one person's opinion. Yes, a thousand times, yes!! This is precisely why we need to ponder scripture, not merely read and quote it. Clearly, it seems to me that the very human people who in antiquity wrote the scripture down believed in an angry and vengeful God. So, thinking that God was angry and vengeful and had to be talked out of acting angrily and without justice by both Moses and Abraham made sense to those scribes, but it doesn't make sense to me. I don't believe in an angry and vengeful God. I believe God, whoever and whatever God may be, is about justice and love, not anger and vengeance. Which takes us again to an approach to scripture of discussion and pondering, not blind obedience and quotation.

As a Jew, I look back at the history of Judaism, and it seems clear that in its early days Judaism indeed embraced the idea of an angry and vengeful God. Today, Judaism views God as a God of love and justice. So, did God change? Personally, I don't think so. I believe it is we who have changed, and as we have changed, how we see the sacred (whether or not we use the word God) has changed as well. When I was younger and into my 50s, I looked at this primarily through the lens of Judaism. But then I received the revelations that pointed me to Interfaith.

Many have spoken for Me. They were righteous and they did carry My words. But I am not human, and you are not God. Language can be a barrier between us as well as yourselves that can be all but impossible to breach. Seek truth in the commonality of religions—which are but the languages of speaking to Me. Worship not the grammar.

After living with this and pondering it, it pointed me to more than simply rethinking my approach to the "grammar" of our differing traditions. The call was to seek truth not in what separates our spiritual traditions but rather in what unites them. This is the heart and soul of Interfaith: seeking truth in the commonality of our diverse religions.

We'll go more deeply into that in the next chapter. For now, what does it point us to in terms of how we deal with scripture? I have consciously dealt above only with Hebrew Scripture. It is the scripture I grew up with and the scripture of my heritage. At this point in my life, age 74, I have read (in translation, of course) the scriptures of many spiritual traditions. I have used the example of my own scripture, the one I am most familiar with, but would invite the reader to ponder and examine the scriptures (sacred writing if scripture becomes a limiting word) of their own spiritual tradition.

For me, our scripture is importantly influenced by the era, culture, and life experience of the believers who received it and wrote it down. Our scriptures, then, are guidebooks, not rulebooks. They are crucially important guides for living a more meaningful life, and not repositories of immovable, unchanging spiritual interpretations from hundreds, and for many of us, thousands of years ago. Perhaps most important, all scripture, *all* scripture is, at its most holy, a translation or, if you will, an interpretation of sacred revelation. Even at its beginning, assuming that the beginning of our holiest passages in scripture was indeed divinely inspired and began as communication from God, it can only be what we imperfect humans have interpreted that Word to be. And that interpretation can change. These differences in interpretation are a major reason why virtually all of our spiritual paths have branches. As but one example that most will be familiar with, in Christianity there are the Catholic and Protestant branches. And there are branches within those branches, all, in large part, from interpreting a common scripture differently. Christianity is, of course, not alone. Judaism has branches, Islam has branches, and so on. This is an important and complex subject, and we'll return to it later.

For now, what this means to me is that I feel called to respect the sacred texts, the guidebooks of all my brothers and sisters, even as I, being

Jewish, cleave to as well as question the guidebooks of my own heritage, all the while remembering that interpretations of these guidebooks can and will vary. This includes the whole of Jewish scripture as well as the additions, qualifications, and reinterpretations made over the centuries as our eras and experiences have changed. This includes particularly but not solely the "Pirke Avot," the wisdom of the fathers, which houses the sacred writings of the rabbis such as Hillel and Tarfon.

So, what truth is available to us by seeking the commonalities of our diverse traditions? And how does this help us to answer the call of Interfaith?

CHAPTER FOUR

The call of Interfaith in no way rejects religion. It is a call to realize that our spiritual traditions are living, breathing entities that change over time, as does all of life. Still, "Seek truth in the commonality of religions, which are but the languages of speaking to Me. Worship not the grammar" took some living with.

I began to imagine a sacred mountain for humanity. At the mountaintop dwelt the call of the sacred, the commonality that would hold the truths to living a meaningful life to which all of our sacred traditions seek to point us. Our differing spiritual traditions would be diverse paths up this sacred mountain that our differing eras and cultures had found helpful.

The "grammar," then, is the particular ritual and practice that formed the glue of our differing paths. Grammar is indeed relevant because it helps to put structure and definition to the paths we walk. That said, for me what calls us to the mountaintop is the sacred truth that dwells there and not the grammar of the particular path we walk. What's important, then, is to *get* to the mountaintop. There have been and still are a multitude of paths to get there, and to my core I believe we are free to choose the path that feels best to us. But whatever path we take, we are called to walk that path with integrity and with our eyes and hearts fixed on that mountaintop where the sacred dwells. Proclaiming our path is not enough. We need to walk it.

So, what is this truth to be found in "the commonality of religions" that dwelt at the mountaintop? To see that meant looking at our multitude of paths without judging. That's hard enough, but I believe it also means something else. I believe there is no single truth that comprises the sacred. I deeply believe that we are *not* called to seek "the" truth in the commonality of religions. Rather, when we believe we have grasped a meaningful truth, we should test it by looking for it in spiritual paths that are not our own.

For me, the great calling that bound me to Judaism was the call of justice. With the reminder that I'm just one person and cannot speak for Judaism, as I studied Judaism as child and then a youth, what bound me to this path of my heritage was the call of justice. I not only believed in acting with justice but also that the call of justice was the call to which I owed my allegiance. I believed in a God of justice. This informed every aspect of my life. Indeed, it was when I saw so much injustice around me that I experienced my spiritual crisis in 1999.

A quick caveat as I explore the four aspects to living a meaningful life that I found at the mountaintop. These are *not* submitted as the only way of interpreting the truths available to us. Rather, these are the components of justice that have called to me all my life and call to me still. These are the truths that I cleave to and that I hope and believe have led me to be a better human being.

Three of these aspects came from the individual who is admittedly my favorite of the prophets: Micah. From Micah 6:4, "And what does Lord require of thee? Only this: to act justly, love compassion, and walk humbly with your God." (A reminder that Hebrew scripture did *not* come to us in English! This is a translation, and, as with all translations, it is an interpretation. More about a particular translation shortly.)

For me, these three things are all crucial, and I realized as I studied what Micah said, that they were not three separate things. They were three crucial components of one thing: living a life of justice. First, we are to ACT justly. Proclaiming how much we value justice falls way short if we will not act justly, but living a life of justice is much more than acting with justice.

We are called to love compassion. Let's be honest here. The word that is usually used in English is "mercy," not compassion, but for me, "mercy" is arrogant compassion. "I'm better than you, bigger than you, and stronger than you, but I will show mercy. Aren't I swell?" No, thanks. Compassion is mercy without arrogance. To love compassion is to realize that we are all in this together and should treat one another like family. This is a crucial part of living a just life.

Finally, we are called to walk humbly with our God. This was first explained to me as God is so great we must be humbled in God's presence. I didn't and don't buy that. I believe and interpret this as a call to walk hand in hand with the sacred while living a life of humility. I should be humble not only in the presence of God but also in the presence of my human family. Indeed, I should walk humbly in the presence of Mother Nature and every stick, stone, flower, and creature on Earth. I deeply believe that there can be no justice without humility. Humility calls on us to treat each other with respect. That, for me, is a crucial aspect of acting with justice.

Still, as important as the words of Micah were and are to me, I found them sharpened and made clearer by another great teacher, Rabbi Shimon, the son of Rabbi Gamaliel. He is reported to have said, "The world stands on three things: on justice, on truth, and on peace." Yes! How can we possibly live with justice, truth, and in peace if we will not treat each other with justice, truth, and peace? And that means community. Our world, then, stands (or falls) on how we value community.

For me, these are the four great aspects of living a just life in harmony with the sacred:

1. Act with justice toward all.
2. Love compassion, and embrace (not "tolerate") community. My life is about us, not me.

3. Embrace compassion as way of interacting with all our human family. Truly, this is to embrace peace. There can be no peace without community. There can be no community without peace. This means peace brought about by the fist is only an illusion of peace. True community comes from oneness, not submission.

4. Walk with humility. Eschew arrogance. When we do well, rejoice! When we falter, resolve to do better. But always, always walk with humility.

These were the four aspects of justice that called to me. But again, the revelation asked me to "Seek truth in the commonality of religions." So my task was to see if these were considered truths in spiritual traditions that were not Jewish.

Having served as the choir director in a Methodist church, as well as having taken "The Bible as Literature" from a minister as an undergraduate in college, I was very much aware of the pivotal position of love, compassion and justice in Christianity. As but one example, from Ephesians 4:25, "Therefore, putting away falsehood, let everyone speak the truth with his neighbor, for we are members one of another."

As I went looking, there it was in the scripture of the Sikh (the Adi Granth): "All humanity shall live in peace with one another, under a shield of justice." In the Qur'an of Islam: "Stand firmly for justice, as witnesses to Allah, even as against yourselves, or your family." And with the Buddhists, the Baha'i, indeed, everywhere I looked, justice and its components—love, compassion, and humility—were not just apparent in our own spiritual traditions; the call to it was repeated over and over again. Which, I must admit, led me to what I call the "vegetable theory of scripture."

When we were children, how often did our parents have to say, "Eat your dessert!"? As adults with children of our own, how often have we had to demand, "Finish your dessert!"? It wasn't "eat your dessert" that we had to repeat over and over, as there was very little need. What was repeated over, and over, and over again was "Eat your vegetables!" Why?

Because kids don't eat their vegetables. As adults, we have the same problem. I like to call this the "vegetable syndrome."

What does this have to do scripture and our spiritual traditions? If we are called, over and over and over again, to act with justice toward one another, to be loving and compassionate toward one another, and to be humble in our interactions, it's because aren't doing it. As with the call to eat our vegetables, we are being "nagged" to be loving and compassionate and to act with justice and humility because humanity remains reluctant to this very day.

It was after I had written my first book, *The Interfaith Alternative*, that I became acquainted with the lovely human being who headed the Interfaith desk at the Scarboro Missions in Canada. Paul McKenna had assembled a wonderful example of the universality of the Golden Rule among our spiritual traditions. I'd like to close this chapter with his Golden Rule poster. I use this inspiring poster with his permission. (published by Scarboro Missions; copyright Paul McKenna 2000).

PART TWO:
Dealing with Death and Dying

CHAPTER FIVE

It wasn't lost on me that the questions that most oppressed my mind and had me angrily demanding answers from God weren't answered until halfway through the revelations that were placed before me. Still, what I desperately needed at that moment of crisis in my life was some kind of handle on death and dying. So, what I gravitated to first were the revelations about these two difficult subjects. I read them, reread them, and lived with them. In all honesty, being open to it required me to reorient my thinking about God as well as life and death—which is a lot to unpack! But it did comfort me and help me to begin to move ahead. Given how spent I felt, this was no small task.

The mind is not the soul. Nor is the body. Sometimes, the mind decays or the body writhes with pain before the soul has left it. That is indeed a tragedy. Weep, but do not despair.

There was indeed a lot to unpack in those few sentences. Still, I received immediate comfort from "Weep, but do not despair." As mentioned previously, my father had tried to teach me from childhood that "real men" don't cry. Ever. He wanted me to embrace that showing sadness, like weeping, was a sign of weakness. Indeed, I can only remember my father crying once. It was when we buried our beloved family dog in our backyard. Dad shed one, maybe two tears, but then quickly wiped them away and apologized to my mother, my sister, and to me for shedding a tear.

My father's teaching had only partially taken. When faced with tragedy, I indeed felt great sadness, but I must admit that I also felt guilty for feeling sad. I tried hard to battle the sadness, to bury it, and in so doing I think I greatly prolonged it. Now here was what I believed was the voice of God telling me that it was both okay to weep and that tragedy is real and should be acknowledged. What a relief! However, this reassuring comfort did not stand alone. "Weep, but do not despair." Don't despair? What did that mean? It seemed to me I was being told that while sadness was indeed the proper and very human response to tragedy, even so, I must not give up. I needed to live my life. No matter what the tragedy, I must not give up. "Weep, but do not despair." As I pondered it, I found this both comforting and empowering.

Nor was this the whole of the revelation. It began with, "The mind is not the soul. Nor is the body. Sometimes, the mind decays or the body writhes with pain before the soul has left it. That is indeed a tragedy." Still sad but no longer despairing, I began to unpack what this might mean. Like many, if not most of us, I'd heard the word *soul* often in my life and almost always as a cliché, or at best a metaphor. "That person has an old soul." And, of course, "that person has sold their soul" for personal gain. Any thinking about what a soul might or might not actually be was rare, and on those rare occasions, short and not particularly deep. Now, I needed to come to grips with it as more than just a metaphor. Here it was—straightforward and unavoidable.

"The mind is not the soul. Nor is the body. Sometimes, the mind decays or the body writhes with pain before the soul has left it."

This laid out clearly to me that there is a part of us that's neither our mind nor our body. Okay. What then? As I've pondered this and lived with the question, I have come to believe that our soul is a piece of Cosmic Conscience (more about God as Cosmic Conscience in the next chapters). For me, our souls are not concerned with eating, or drinking, or exercise, or touch. *Not* that these things aren't important if we want to continue living and enjoy that life! But they are the concerns of our body. Our souls are not concerned with when we get up in the morning, what kind of learning we gain in our lifetimes, whether we should drive when the roads are icy, or when we should pick up groceries. *Not* that these things aren't important if we are to have any order and make any sense of our lives! But they are the concerns of our mind.

As I pondered it, I concluded that our soul is concerned with our conscience, our sense of right and wrong and perhaps most especially, do we live a "me-centric" or an "us-centric" life? More than that, it became clear that what is most central to who we are is our soul. And a soul knows no race, religion, gender, or ethnicity. If we can understand and embrace this, it shatters all attempts at division that our minds concoct.

Beyond this, if indeed the soul exists as separate from our mind and body, the question arises: where does it go when it leaves? What happens to the soul once the mind and body have died?

Oh, that! It's a good and difficult question! We'll examine the answer I've come to, after living with it and pondering it for years, in the next chapter. Still, it's important to stress that it's simply (or not so simply) the answer that the revelations led *me* to. It's one answer. It's the one I've embraced, but is by no means offered here as the only answer. Other folks may well disagree with me. And the one thing we know for sure is that there is no way to know for sure!! For me, one of the great frustrations, indeed, tragedies of our human history is that we have constantly sought to embrace one "right" answer, one simple answer, to this hugely difficult question and then shut down any further thought.

Many of us believe that there is life after death. We may well get into passionate arguments with one another over the nature of that life after death, but uniting all of this group is the belief that there is *some* kind of life. The truth of it is, however, that there is no proof that there *is* life after death.

Many of us believe that there is no such thing as life after death. When we die, that's it. Body, mind, and whatever the soul is as well: done. Worm food. But the truth of it is, there is no proof of this, either. There is no proof that there is *no* life after death.

I think Shakespeare got it right in his play *"Hamlet"* when Hamlet describes death as, "That undiscovered country from whose bourn no traveler returns." It indeed puzzles the mind. The hard truth is that we don't know. We can guess. We can believe. But we don't know.

For me, our seeming inability to live without knowing is indeed tragic. Admitting that we don't know seems somehow to offend our innate arrogance in how we approach life. We would rather come up with an "answer," some answer, *any* answer and then be willing to divide ourselves bitterly over whose answer—to something we cannot possibly know—is the one "right" answer. And from that spew millennia of bigotry, hate, fear, and, much too often, violence. All this over something we cannot know.

I approached and approach this discussion of death as an agnostic. I don't know. When I look at and ponder what was revealed to me, I can interpret what I heard, and indeed I do interpret it. Moreover, that interpretation is what I now deeply believe, but at the same moment I want to acknowledge that another person may interpret those same words differently. For me, I do not believe the soul ceases to exist when the body and mind have died. That's how I interpret what was shared. But if the soul does not cease to exist, what then?

You cannot live forever, but you can be with Me forever. Time is your measure, not Mine.

This, too, was comforting. The souls of those beloved people whose lives had been cut short could be with God forever. But with the comfort came the question, what did it mean? Okay, their souls hadn't just disappeared, simply ceased to exist. But what did it mean to "be" with "Me"? Assuming, as I did, that "Me" was God, what did it mean to be with God? Heaven? Were we talking about heaven? If so, then what did that mean? And if not, then how else might a soul "be" with God?

CHAPTER SIX

For me, while the thought of a soul being with God forever was indeed warmly comforting, the idea of a soul dwelling in, or confined to, a gated heaven was not. I'd grown up and indeed lived most of my life surrounded by people who talked about heaven's "pearly gates." Heaven as a gated community? The image was perfect—perfectly horrible. Only the "anointed" need apply. And who was the guardian of the gates, checking off who would be admitted and who would be turned away? Peter, a white male Christian saint. No, thanks. I've never liked gated communities on Earth. I certainly wasn't interested in one for our souls.

So, what to do with, "You cannot live forever, but you can be with Me forever."? If religion is but a language for speaking to and about God, then a gated community of believing souls made no sense. So, what did make sense?

To get there, it became much clearer to me that I needed a better understanding of God. And yes, that took time—a lot of time. It also took a rather firm push. I got that push in a class given by a professor at the School of Theology and Ministry at Seattle University when I was studying to be a minister there. Our required paper was to put who and what we believed God to be into words. What made the paper so helpful was that the professor made it clear that he wasn't looking for a "right answer." What he wanted us to do was to be clear about what we believed and then carefully explore what the implications of that belief were. What a wonderful teacher!

By then, I'd been living with and pondering the revelations for more than five years, without ever coming to a clear understanding of how I saw God. Now I needed to put it into words, and as I pondered it, the thoughts that had been swirling around in my heart and brain at last came pouring out.

Who or what had reached out to me when I was crying out for answers? I believed then and believe now that it was God. But what do I mean by that? I realized that had I been Muslim I would have perceived the enlightenment as from Allah. I also realized that the Buddha had received his enlightenment without believing that he had heard from God. Okay. If I believed in seeking truth in the commonality of all of our spiritual traditions, how to include not only my own Judaism, but Christianity, Islam, Buddhism, and Humanism, among so many differing ways of perceiving spirit?

The more I pondered it, the more I saw the call of the sacred in all of our spiritual traditions as a call to morality (though the call clearly can manifest itself quite differently): the call of justice, compassion, love, and community. How to put that into language?

After all this time, the honest truth is that I do not *know* who God is or where God dwells. What I believe is that there is a moral core to the universe and that it has tried its best to communicate with me, as I have done my best to understand it. I experience that moral core as God. God may not be human, but I am. And my ability to understand the revelations shared is limited by that.

In receiving and then pondering the revelations, it seemed to me that I was dealing with some kind of Cosmic Conscience. Can't I be more exact than that? No, I can't. Whatever had reached out to me, I wrote down what I heard in my head, but to be able to write it down, I had to interpret it. Because I speak English, that's what I heard and what I wrote. But I don't believe that God is an English speaker any more than a speaker of Hebrew, Latin, or any other language.

Thus, it became clear to me that I experienced God as Cosmic Conscience, not as a "creator" of the heaven and Earth and not as a miracle maker who can defy the laws of physics at will. I did not see God as male or female but did see God as a timeless, compassionate call to our souls that echoed across the universe—an abiding, loving, and cosmic call to justice and community. This same call was to Jews in the desert, to Christians living under the yoke of Rome, to Muhammad, and the Buddha, and so many others equally. *Equally*! How we perceive that call to conscience will be different according to our culture and era; yet, the call remains the same and has remained constant for millennia. So, if we are not to be separated from the sacred and want to "be" with God forever, what counts is not the specifics of our spiritual tradition but how we answer the call to conscience, how we integrate it into our lives—or don't. Have we done our best, our admittedly fallible human best, to act with justice, to love compassion, and to embrace our human community as we walk humbly with however we define and view the sacred?

Perhaps, then, God didn't create us in God's image. Perhaps we arrogant humans created God in our image. Some have used this possibility to argue that there is no God. I don't. My belief, as it has evolved, as I have learned and listened, is not that humanity invented God but rather that we have anthropomorphized God because we humans are far more comfortable making the sacred look like us than we are dealing with the unknown and perhaps unknowable.

It occurred to me, and still echoes in my heart and mind, that perhaps what Abraham heard was the sacred call of Cosmic Conscience, a call that included justice for Sodom and Gomorrah. Perhaps it was the call of Cosmic Conscience to lead his people from slavery that Moses heard. Perhaps what Jesus heard was the clarion call of abiding love and justice. And so on, including the Buddha, Muhammad, Bahaullah, Black Elk, and so many others—both the famous and so many not known to us. Contemplating this, the life and words of the Buddha in particular called to me.

As I explored Buddhism, we seemed to have a lot in common (to be clear, I'm no expert and cannot speak for Buddhism). While there are indeed differences, these differences seem to be cultural—a different way of expressing the same vision of the call to each of us made by Cosmic Conscience. As I read about Nirvana and that some souls are reborn, almost always several times before reaching Nirvana, I wondered if perhaps Nirvana is the Buddhist interpretation of becoming one with Cosmic Conscience.

Might then having our souls reborn be another opportunity to find our way to be one with the eternal call to justice, compassion, and community? If we answer the call of Cosmic Conscience, the call of God, then perhaps this is what it means for our souls to walk with God. If we will become part of that Cosmic Conscience, then perhaps that is what is meant that our souls can be with God forever. No heaven needed. No gated community required. Rather, when our minds and bodies die and our soul leaves the Earth, we can become one with the cosmic call to love, justice, and community that is God.

But, I now ponder, perhaps there was a time when heaven was needed, when a gated community was required. Both early Jews and Christians lived in a hugely different era. There were no telescopes. There was nothing to tell our brothers and sisters of that era that those twinkling lights in the sky were in fact stars, and that there were galaxies out there. They lived at a time when it was believed that just above our earthly horizon God or the gods dwelt. The Earth didn't orbit the Sun. The Sun orbited the Earth. The ancient Greeks thought that Apollo stashed the Sun in his chariot and rode it across the sky. The ancient Hebrews didn't think of the Sun being moved by a chariot but that God both moved the Sun around the Earth and could stop it at will (and did stop it at least once, at Joshua's bidding; Joshua 10:13). So, the ancients thought the idea of heaven was real, and perhaps early Christians, suffering under the severe lash of Rome, needed to believe in a gated community in heaven, a refuge from the violence on Earth.

When I understood this, another revelation was made clear.

You have misconstrued hell and heaven. Those who separate themselves from Me in life will be separated from Me in death. No more. No less.

If, then, we would not be separated from God, we need to attend to the nurturing of our souls and an embrace of the sacred truths that dwell at the top of our sacred mountain: love, compassion, justice, community.

It is, then, humanity who has created the hell of fire and brimstone, as we've created hell on Earth with witch-burnings and crusades, over and over again with our arrogance and violent self-righteousness. God makes clear: there is no hell other than separation from God's call to embrace conscience, which, as far as I can see, is nothing like the hell humanity has created out of our greed, arrogance, and a consuming quest for power.

I believe that the person who would condemn us to hell—rabbi, imam, minister, priest, or other—is condemning him/herself and no one else. We do, however, condemn ourselves when we follow such people. As Jesus told us, "Let the one who is without sin cast the first stone." And as none of us is perfect, we really do need to stop our stone-throwing.

We are cautioned,

I have imbued every religion with truth. You have imbued every religion with magic[1].

The truth of it is, we like miracles. Throughout human history, it has been so much easier to deal with miracles than to eat our veggies and answer the call of Cosmic Conscience. But we can do it. It's up to us.

I'd close this chapter with this rather stark but at the same time beautiful statement,

---

1. This is the one and only revelation that I've "edited". When I first wrote it down, I wrote "mysticism". I explain why I changed "mysticism" to magic" in "*One Family: Indivisible,*" page 163. In short, I believe that at the time I made no difference in my mind between magic and mysticism. When I later realized that my understanding of mysticism was inaccurate, I changed the word in the revelation to what it reads now: "magic."

Ye who seek to live forever shall die. Ye who seek to live well shall crumble. Ye who seek to live in harmony with all shall know what it is to be blessed.

For me, to be blessed is for our souls to be with God, for our souls to dwell with and indeed be a part of Cosmic Conscience forever. A blessing indeed. Though I'm sure it will come as no surprise that to gain such a blessing involves work—a lot of it. Indeed, it requires a lifetime's worth. We'll explore broad categories of the work we are called to in the chapters that follow. But first, let us examine a bit more closely some revelations about how we might prepare ourselves to be one with Cosmic Conscience.

CHAPTER SEVEN

So, whether we use the word *heaven* or embrace another word, how might we prepare ourselves to "be" with God? IS there any way to prepare ourselves? For me, three of the revelations seemed to speak directly to that.

Cleanse yourselves. Jesus, Moses, Muhammad, the Buddha, they all can provide you soap, but yours is the responsibility for cleansing yourself.

This seems to me both a call to Interfaith and, more important for this chapter, a call to action. The path to a life driven by conscience is neither simple nor easy. If it were, the call to conscience wouldn't have had to be repeated over and over again throughout human history. What do Jesus, Moses, Muhammad, the Buddha, and so many others have in common? Is it not the call to love one another, to act with justice toward all, and to act in community rather than exclude the "stranger" who is seen as "not one of us?"

I believe we will only hear the call of conscience if we are truly open to it. In all of our spiritual traditions, some of us turn a deaf ear to conscience. That's our choice. Those of us who are open to the call of conscience will hear it. Even so, hearing it is insufficient. It is *answering* that call that is so important, and again it is up to us. To be clear, then, conscience is not a call to "behave." It is a call to act with love, compassion, and justice in community with our human family.

Any and every Jew, Christian, Muslim, Buddhist, Baha'i, Humanist, Sikh, and member of any and every spiritual path can turn a deaf ear to the call of conscience. Or we can heed it. It is always our choice.

So, Jesus, Moses, Muhammad, the Buddha, and so many other spiritual leaders, can provide us the "soap." But soap is not enough. Possessing the soap is only a good start. The responsibility for cleansing ourselves remains ours. Still, beyond the metaphor, what does cleansing ourselves mean? Do we have guidance in this? Yes.

You cannot value wealth and love Me. You cannot worship power and be welcome in My home.

We can value wealth or we can value the call of conscience, but not both. We can worship power, or we can be welcomed into the arms of Cosmic Conscience, but not both. This is hardly new! It's what Jesus, Hillel, Bahaullah, the Buddha, Krishna, Muhammad, and so many others have shared with us over and over again. Here are but a few examples (with thanks to *World Scripture* and *One Heart*).

"Again I tell you, it is easier for a camel to go through the eye of a needle than for a rich man to enter the kingdom of God." Christianity (Matthew 19.24) "What good will it be for you if you gain the whole world, yet forfeit your soul?" Christianity (Matthew 6.26)

"If you cultivate wealth, you give up humanity. If you cultivate humanity, you give up wealth." Confucianism (Mencius III.A.3)

"What avail riches for the practice of religion?" Jainism (Uttaradhyayana Sutra 14.16)

"Your worldly riches are transitory, but Allah's reward is everlasting." Islam (Qur'an 16.95)

"He who loves money will never be satisfied with money; nor he who loves wealth be satisfied with gain. This too is vanity." Judaism (Ecclesiastes 5.9-10)

Our diverse spiritual traditions have indeed given us the soap, but just standing around with soap in our hands accomplishes nothing. We need to move from platitude to practice. We have to act. And before we start pointing fingers at others, it seems to me that we first need to cleanse the scum from our own lives.

A good place to start is realizing that our worship of wealth has come to overwhelm almost every other aspect of our culture. We have a culture that idolizes wealth, and by extension a culture that worships or at the very least idolizes the wealthy. This culture calls us to do whatever we can to become wealthy and holds up the wealthiest among us as people to be envied and admired—who is among the top ten wealthiest people in the world and who was but isn't now?

I believe an important part of our soulful cleansing is realizing that particularly at this time of climate catastrophe, COVID upheaval (among so many health concerns), extreme poverty, hunger, and seemingly endless ills among our human family, a person of wealth who clings to that wealth is ignoring the call of conscience and is *not* to be admired. To be sure, there are some people of wealth who are actively giving that wealth away to help deal with these human travails. MacKenzi Scott is one such person, and I deeply admire her. Sadly, however, such people are the exception, not the rule. If we would change that rule, we need to cleanse our own acceptance of greed and leave behind us the belief that wealth is something to be sought and envied.

That said, most of us aren't wealthy and will never be wealthy. Are we out of the picture? No. Each of us is called on to take every action we can in support of conscience. Let's close this chapter by unpacking a revelation that is for me both consoling and challenging.

Love life. Cherish it. Seek to make life better for all within your ability to do so. But life is only a beginning. You but crawl. Do not despise yourselves for crawling but never fear or forget that as a loving parent I hope one day to walk with you.

What does it mean, then, for our souls to walk with God? The call of conscience is clear. "Seek to make life better for all within your ability to do so." This statement itself is both a challenge and a comfort. It's a challenge for we are called to seek to make life better not only for ourselves and immediate family but *all* within our ability to do so. This will mean different things to different folks. To me, it has meant marching for causes when I was physically able to do so, speaking up at city council and county council meetings when I felt the good of the people who lived in my community was at stake, and most especially donating as much as I could to as many charitable causes as I could. I've been doing this for years. Even so, I fully recognize that I haven't changed the huge problems that confront humanity. I may have helped some people and am so very glad to have had that opportunity, but the problems remain. Still, there is comfort in the phrase "within your power to do so." None of us is tasked with saving the world on our own! What we are tasked with is seeking to make life better for all within our ability to do so. And, of course, it doesn't end there.

Lest we become overwhelmed and discouraged by the magnitude of what needs to be done: "But life is only a beginning. You but crawl. Do not despise yourselves for crawling, but never fear or forget that as a loving parent I hope one day to walk with you."

For me, this is huge. "Do not despise yourselves for crawling." It doesn't say, "It's too big, stop crawling!" The call of conscience demands of us that we do what we can, whatever "what we can" may be. Even if we are merely crawling, crawl forward! And however little what we can do appears to us to be, we are lovingly told, "Do not despise yourselves for crawling." More than that, we are told, "But never fear or forget that as a loving parent I hope one day to walk with you."

Okay, fine. What does *that* mean?? Clearly, it's open to many interpretations. Does God actually hope to stroll somewhere with us? Some can, and indeed have interpreted this in precisely that literal manner. I see it differently. I would offer my interpretation not as "the" correct interpretation. Rather, it is offered as one possible interpretation, and it is indeed the one I cleave to.

Seeing God as Cosmic Conscience and seeing our souls as at least potentially becoming a part of this cosmic call to conscience when our minds and bodies die, I see God hoping one day to walk with us as God hoping that we choose the path of conscience and indeed actively walk the path of conscience. If we do, then we have entered the "heaven" that was spoken of in the previous chapter – not a physical heaven, but a state of "being" with God. In that sense, Cosmic Conscience is the parent of our own conscience—if we will nurture rather than neglect or ignore it.

In the next three sections, we'll explore more fully what I have come to see as the three great calls to conscience: the call to love one another, the call to justice, and the call to community.

PART THREE:
The Call to Love One Another

CHAPTER EIGHT

If there is anything that our diverse spiritual traditions agree on, it's the foundational call for us to love one another. It is not that we have been called to be loving once or twice but that we have been called over and over, throughout the centuries, in all of our traditions. Most of us will be familiar with this call from Jewish and Christian sources. Perhaps most famously:

"The foreigner who sojourns with you shall be unto you as the native-born, and you shall love that person as you love yourself—for you were a foreigner in the land of Egypt." (Leviticus: 19.34)

And ...

"Beloved, let us love one another; for love is of God." (I John 4.7)

These are, of course, but the tips of a loving iceberg. The call to love is repeated again and again in Judaism, and, of course, as Jesus' "great commandment," over and over in Christianity.

However, the call to be loving, the repeated call to be loving, emerges from all of our traditions. All of them. Before launching into that, however, it might be helpful to be a little clearer about what we mean, at least here, when we say, "Love." I trust we all acknowledge that we're not talking about romance. What we are talking about is compassion—active compassion. To be loving is not a passive pursuit.

With that understanding, here are but a few examples (in translation). They are, again, only the tip of the loving iceberg that has engaged the world. The call to love is both rich and universal (quotes below from my own knowledge as well as *World Scripture* and *One Heart*).

Baha'i: "It is not for him to pride himself who loveth his own country, but rather for him who loveth the whole world." (Bahaullah – Gleanings: 117)

Buddhism: "As a mother guards the life of her child with her own life, embrace all that lives as thine own." (Metta Sutta)

Hinduism: "You must show compassion to all living beings. Compassion is the root of all faiths." (Basava – Vachana)

Taoism: "Love the world as you love yourself; then you can truly care for all things." (Tao Te Ching 13)

Islam: "Those who act with compassion in the world will have compassion." (Qur'an 39.10)

Native American spirituality: "It makes no difference what name we give to God, for Love is the true god of the entire world." (Apache proverb)

For more examples, do take another look at the wonderful poster at the end of Part One that exemplifies the worldwide embrace of the Golden Rule. The call to love one another and to treat our neighbor as we would be treated is indeed universal. So when I received this among the revelations granted to me, it was certainly nothing new.

You cannot love Me and hate your neighbor.

No, nothing new. So, why was it needed? I believe it was and is needed for the simple and deeply saddening reason that however many times we have received this call to be loving, humanity continues to ignore it—year after year, century after century, millennium after millennium. This takes us back to the "vegetable syndrome" we discussed in Part One. Parents don't need to say to their kids, "Eat your dessert." Most parents, perhaps the overwhelming majority, *do* need to say, "Eat your vegetables." They have to say it over and over. Why? Because kids are *still* not eating their vegetables, no matter how many times their caring parents have pleaded with them. Why has humanity needed to hear over and over again the call to love one another? It's because after all these years we still succumb to the call of our emotional sweet tooth: greed, social importance, personal comfort, fear of insignificance, and the desire to control others, among so many other temptations. Each pulls us away from the repeated call to compassion. "You cannot love Me and hate your neighbor." Here's a thought. Perhaps it's time we not only listened but actually made these words central to our lives.

I believe this means making the call to active love, to the compassionate embracing of our human family, more than a proclamation. To be honest, I've lost count of the number of times throughout human history people have loudly proclaimed the primacy of love—while practicing arrogant feelings of supremacy, frequently accompanied by bigotry, hate, and violence. At this very moment, we can see that bigotry, hatred and violence are rampant in the world around us. If we are to answer the call of love, it seems to me the first step is to recognize that love involves our action, not our words.

Frankly, I've also lost count of the instances in my own lifetime when I've heard the equivalent of a person saying (individually, or as TV clergy addressing the audience), "I believe in a God of love. God is this, not this. God is this, not this. God is this, not this. And either you embrace the God of love that I describe and believe in, or my God of love will hate you and cast you into hell, with me cheering from the sidelines." Really? If that's what we truly believe, then our God of love is not very loving, and neither are we! And again, this is nothing new.

Confucius recognized it some 2,600 years ago! In the "Doctrine of the Mean," Confucianism sums up not only the universality of the call of conscience but also that humanity keeps missing it. Here are Confucius' words on the call of conscience—moral law as he calls it. "The moral law is to be found everywhere, and yet it is a secret." Well, I'd beg to quibble just a bit with Confucius' wording. Moral law is not secret so much as we keep closing our eyes to it.

Why? Here are some thoughts—not definitive answers, but some thoughts.

I believe G. K. Chesterton, writing in the early 20th century, hit the nail firmly on the head. He wrote, "The Christian ideal has not been tried and found wanting. It has been found difficult and not tried." My only disagreement here is that this failure applies to all of our spiritual traditions, not just Christianity. As Confucius found, if I may paraphrase, the moral law is everywhere: spoken and lifted high, then hidden away and ignored.

For far too many of us, the call of "peace on Earth, good will to all" seems to be terrifying. Good will to all? To all? If we feel unworthy and uncomfortable with our value as human beings, we may feel compelled to put others down in order to lift ourselves up. I still recall as a teenager when an anguished acquaintance, who knew his bigotry was wrong, plaintively justified it by saying, "I have to be better than *somebody*!" And this takes us to the painful question of meaning. What, if anything, does our time on this planet signify?

In his play, "Man of La Mancha," playwright Dale Wasserman has Cervantes say that he has held comrades who had fallen in battle, "… their eyes filled with confusion, whimpering the question 'Why?' I do not think they asked why they were dying, but why they had lived."

This question of why we have lived has plagued humanity from the time we first were able to think. What are we to make of our lives? What is the point? Where do we find meaning? I believe this is the wrong question as I do not believe that we will ever "find" meaning. I believe that meaning is lived, not found. This bears repeating. Meaning is *lived*, not found. Thus, our "search for meaning" is a lifelong task. As long as we do not give up on ourselves on living meaningfully, meaning can and, I hope, will be our companion—our companion, not our possession. Meaning will walk with us only so long as we walk with meaning.

Our beliefs cannot give us meaning for meaning cannot be given. What our beliefs can do is guide us to act meaningfully. So, yet again, it's not our beliefs but the actions those beliefs prompt that can, if we indeed will act lovingly, help guide us to live a meaningful life.

In closing, we are not called to love only those who agree with us, or who pray like us, or look like us. We are called to love our neighbor, whoever that neighbor might be, and however that neighbor might look. We are called to love the stranger, whoever that stranger might be, and however that stranger might look. It's a life lived with compassion for all of our human family, not just ourselves and/or our own small group, that brings us both closer to Cosmic Conscience and to souls that have lived meaningfully, however long those souls have dwelt on Earth.

It is then, not how long we live or how comfortably we live, but how lovingly we live. It's a journey—a lifelong task. Let us join hands and walk together lovingly. Let us do this for ourselves, for our children, for posterity.

CHAPTER NINE

This chapter continues the conversation by addressing two seemingly contradictory revelations—seemingly contradictory, but, in fact, they are revelations that I believe are in complete harmony with one another. Let's start with the final revelation I received. I believe it extremely powerful and important.

I speak not to command, but so you may know.

Such a simple statement, but with so much packed within it.

Crucial to this, I believe, is a call to let go the notion of an "all-powerful, all-knowing, jealous and angry God," Let it rest with our ancestors. It's how they experienced the world. It was valid for them and not to be made light of. Still, it's not our world. Not today. Not when we know that our Earth is a very small planet in a huge galaxy that is but one out of millions upon millions of galaxies in our universe.

To this day, I hear some folks lament what they see as the "absence" of God in today's world. Why, they ask, did God perform so many miracles in ancient times but so few today? Often they will quote scripture, written 2,000 years ago, that God knows all, even of the fall of the smallest sparrow. So, if God knows all, why is God now so ambivalent regarding humanity and the Earth, only willing to intervene on occasion, and only if we pray "just right"?

Consider what this implies. If we are praying that our sick child recover and don't use precisely the "right" wording, God will ignore us? Is this the "loving" God we believe in?

I wish I could remember more, but a moment at a service I attended when I was in my 20s is burned into my mind—nothing before or after that moment, but the moment itself. Some teens had been in a traffic accident the week before. At least one of them had died, and at least one had survived. The mother of a teen who lived spoke up at the service, thanking God for sparing her child and proclaiming proudly that clearly God had plans for her child. The moment that is burned into my soul is the palpable gasp and anguished cry of another mother at the service. I discovered after the service that her child had died in that same accident. And here was the first mother saying that God had made a decision that only her child would live and that the other child would die. Why? Because God had plans for one of the children but not the other child? The other child could be discarded with the day's trash?

For me, this was a body blow. Among other things, it was starkly clear to me that this could not be the God of love I believed in. The God I cleave to would both rejoice at the life that was saved and grieve over the life that was lost. A clearer understanding of this would come later. At the time, what it told me was that something was terribly wrong in how we perceive God. Only decades later would the revelations at last make things clear to me.

"I speak not to command, but so you may know."

This demanded a lot of thought from me. In the end, it took me back to scripture and helped me to understand it lot more clearly. It brought me to the understanding that our scriptures are indeed important—not as the unerring Word of God and God's commandments, but as repositories of human understanding of Cosmic Conscience, that our scriptures are guides and not to be taken literally. This explained a lot.

We talked briefly earlier about the various branches of our spiritual traditions, but how could there be differing branches if scripture is the unerring Word of God? And how can the unerring Word of God be so different in differing scriptures? My first introduction to this question concerned Christianity. First came Rome and Catholic Orthodox Christianity.

With the same scripture, however, there soon developed Greek Orthodox Christianity. It didn't stop, however, with the two branches. Starting with Martin Luther, in the late 15th and early 16th centuries, Protestant Christianity emerged. Soon the Protestant Reformation swept much of Europe, and the two competing branches of Christianity now began to war. Europe's Wars of Religion (from the 16th to mid-17th centuries) were fought over the very same scripture—whose primary teaching was and is love.

The branching of Christianity didn't stop there. After Luther and Lutherans, came Methodists, Baptists, and many others. Nor, of course, is this limited to Christianity. Islam holds Sunni, Shia, Ismaili, and many others. Judaism holds Orthodox, Conservative, Reform and many others. How can this be if scripture is the unalterable Word of God and God's commandments? "I speak not to command, but so you may know." Aha! Scripture, then, is *not* a book of commandments, but scriptural guides. And these guides, though inspired by God, are human translations of God's Word.

That they are translations is important. Jesus did not speak English. Nor did Moses, nor the Buddha, Muhammad, Bahaullah, or Confucius, among so many. We see translations of what they said, and their words themselves were translations by very human beings into their own languages of what they had heard from the Divine. Why do we keep speaking about translations? Because translations can change.

"Thou shalt not kill" might also be translated "Thou shalt not murder." Is all taking of life murder? Is killing for food murder? Is killing for sport murder? Are executions murder? Different people will interpret this differently, which is the point. If we will interpret our scriptures as guides, not commandments, we can disagree without resorting to hate and violence. This takes me back to the study of Torah, as preached by so many rabbis. Study it, discuss it, perhaps argue about it from time to time, always remembering that there is no final word.

God, then, reaches out to us to provide loving guidance. Whether or not we act on that guidance is up to us. It is our choice. God indeed loves us and, if we will listen and *act* on what we hear, Cosmic Conscience will indeed reach out to help and guide us. This is how scripture can help us. But God does not utter unalterable commandments from on high. Oh, really? Then what to make of this?

THIS is My commandment. Seek none harm. Love the diversity of your brothers and sisters.

For me, this is God saying, "I don't do commandments. I am here to love and guide you. But if you *must* have a commandment, if you insist on a commandment then okay, take this. Take this *one* 'commandment,' hold it next to your hearts and burn it into your souls. 'Love the diversity of your brothers and sisters.' Don't let diversity divide you! Live lives of love, welcoming diversity, not fearing it!"

For me, then, as I ponder this today, I interpret the "commandment" as a statement that "THIS is what is important. This is what matters." Indeed, "this" is the cornerstone of the call of Cosmic Conscience. It is the cornerstone of a life lived in concert with conscience. It is a life lived in companionship with meaning.

But a call to love? Again? We heard it the first thousand times! Why does it keep being repeated! Perhaps it keeps being repeated because we repeatedly ignore it. For me, one of the great tragedies of human history has been that so often in arguing so vehemently over "why" we should love one another, we have learned to hate one another. In arguing over why we should treat each other with justice and compassion we have learned to act with injustice and even violence.

Looking at human history, what I take from this is that God does not command. God guides. God reaches out to us, if we will listen, with guidance, with what Confucius called moral law. Commandments come from dictators and would-be dictators. Commandments come from people seeking wealth, power, and dominion over others, who turn their interpretation of moral law into commandments. Why? Because, by odd coincidence, once guidance is perverted into unalterable stone commandments, the people in charge, or the people who take charge, can use and abuse them as they see fit.

Far too often, today as it has been for centuries, any difference between us has become a value judgment in our culture, as well as a path to power and wealth for those who seek to manipulate us. "Oh, you drive a Chevy? I drive a Ford." This is an observation, not an attack on people who drive a Chevy unless it profits someone to make it so. "Oh, you like oranges? I prefer peas." Again, this is an observation, not an attack on oranges, or on you for liking them, unless it profits someone to make it so. Yet, in today's polarized world, we readily divide into Ford or Chevy people, orange or pea people.

In the same vein, and far more tragically, we divide over the "right" way to believe, the "right" way to pray, the "right" way to view the divine. We divide, and then we learn to hate and even to commit violence.

Who benefits from this? We don't. Those who benefit are those who are in power and want to stay in power, or those not in power who seek to use these divisions as their path to dominance.

It doesn't stop with our spiritual differences. There are many, far too many, who seek to divide us by race. We are one family, and it's time, long past time, to act like it.

Regardless of race, gender, geographical location, or spiritual tradition, what is important is not why we act with love, even if the "why" differs from person to person. What is important is that we in fact **act** with love.

Okay, so how on Earth do we accomplish this miracle? There's no single answer, not to a problem this complex and with such staying power. But here is one answer: we could start coming together in loving Interfaith congregations.

I've been saying this for some time, and frequently I hear back, "Good grief! If there's one thing we don't need, it's another religion." My reply remains, Interfaith is a way of coming together to understand and heal. It is *not* a new religion, nor does it seek to become one.

Interfaith congregations are not about finding the one "right" answer. Indeed, at least for me, Interfaith congregations are not about worship. They are about embracing the sacred: love and compassion in community, guided by justice. An Interfaith congregation becomes a place of renewal, where we not only reconnect with each other, but by respecting and engaging our diversity, we have the opportunity to reconnect with all of humanity.

This goes back to the pivotal, "I speak not to command but so you many know." God seeks to guide us—if we will listen. The call of Cosmic Conscience is clear. It is not made up of lines in the sand. It is not made up of words that were interpreted thousands of years ago and will never be allowed to grow as humanity grows. It is NOT made up of immovable commandments. The call of Cosmic Conscience is the call to see all of humanity as our family, and to treat our family, the entirety of our human family, with love.

In other words, "For crying out loud, let's eat our vegetables."

Part Four:
The Call to Justice

CHAPTER TEN

I can't explain it, but from the earliest years I can remember, the call of justice has been the cornerstone value of my life. That said, like many of us, if not most, I never really spent a lot of time pondering what exactly justice meant. It seemed lodged within me that the crux of it was this: justice was doing right and being treated right; injustice was doing wrong and being treated wrongly. In terms of the divine, I felt that justice was getting the life we deserved and injustice was getting a life we did not deserve. With benefit of hindsight, this was rather biblical but not a particularly nuanced approach.

Still, it was the stark divine injustice that I saw happening to people so close and important to me that sparked the eruption of my angry demand for answers from God. The love of my life had been killed in a meaningless traffic accident. My mother got to enjoy only a few wonderful years of self-knowledge when cancer took her life. The final straw was my father. While I disagreed with him on some important things (like flaming patriarchy), he had still lived the best life he could, dedicating himself to helping people as best as his patriarchal blinders allowed. He died a humiliating death, starkly aware that dementia was robbing him of his mind as cancer took his life. And there was much more. My hero, Dr. Martin Luther King Jr., had been assassinated. Both Bobby and Jack Kennedy had been assassinated. Peacemakers Anwar al-Sadat and Yitzhak Rabin had been assassinated, Sadat by a "fellow Muslim" and Rabin by a "fellow Jew." There's justice in this world? The God of Israel was a God of justice? Really? So where the heck was justice?

In all honesty, I was angrily demanding answers from a God that at the time I wasn't sure actually existed. But if God were there, and if God were indeed a God of justice, I wanted answers. And, as we've seen, I got answers and then some. As I pondered those answers in the months and indeed years that followed, a lot of things changed in my mind and heart.

For one thing, the God I experienced in the revelations was clearly not the puppet-master God, pulling the strings of creation, that I'd been taught of in religious school. The God I experienced was indeed a God of justice, but that justice flowed from Cosmic Conscience. This meant not only rethinking how I looked at God but also how I saw justice. It was something that indeed took a lot of time and deep thought.

So what *is* justice? Good question. I realized I'd never really spent the time to pin it down. Now, nudged rather firmly by the revelations, I took the time.

For me, the Oxford English Dictionary (OED) has always been a favorite place to start a word hunt. It presented me with five, somewhat related though differing definitions. The first definition was "uprightness." Second, "equity." Third was "vindication of right." Fourth came "administration of law." Last on the list was "infliction of punishment." I could easily live with and embrace the first four. The fifth definition rankled. It had rankled me from my first encounter with it as a student though I was now certainly pleased that it ranked fifth!

That said, my own scripture defined justice as "infliction of punishment." Exodus 21:23-24: "…life for life, eye for eye, tooth for tooth, hand for hand, foot for foot." For me, that's vengeance, not justice. I deeply felt and feel to this day that the two are *not* the same. So, once again I found myself in conflict with what some (certainly not all) of my religious school teachers had laid out.

Fairly early in my public-school life, I was introduced to the Code of Hammurabi (dating about 1750 BCE). It, too, I was taught, laid down the law of an eye for an eye. Only much later did I learn that the Code of Hammurabi also preached equity and that its stated purpose was to protect the weak from the strong. So what did protecting the weak from the strong have to do with mindless (my perspective) vengeance?

In truth, I discovered as I began my life as a choral director in the Methodist Church (again, for context please see "*One Family: Indivisible*") that I found myself much more comfortable with the Christian approach expressed in Romans 12:17-21, which concluded by saying. "Never avenge yourselves, but leave it to the wrath of God; for it is written 'Vengeance is mine, I will repay, saith the Lord.' ... Do not be overcome by evil, but overcome evil with good."

I still had plenty of questions about the wrath of God, but it was good to have it laid out that revenge wasn't our province. This was confirmed in the Jewish Torah commentaries I studied later (see particularly the work of Hillel, among many others). It became clear that at the time of Jesus, and even before, Judaism was moving away from seeing justice as vengeance and more toward acting justly in the world. And acting justly was seen as acting with moral integrity.

Still, where was God in all of this? Was God to be seen as an actor of vengeance in the world? Or was God to be seen as an actor upholding righteousness? I not only struggled with that but also with the realization that if God was to be seen as upholding righteousness in the world, then where was God when there was so much lack of righteousness? Where was God during the Shoah/Holocaust was a question that had been discussed, with no real answer, in many conversations I had with fellow students and teachers in religious school. Yet this begged what was for me an even more important question. Justice doesn't concern only Jews! Where was God with all the injustice that had happened to so many throughout history? Where was God with all the injustice to be found in the modern world?

At some point (I think, but can't be certain that it was while I was in college) I heard and was deeply moved by a wonderful and deeply poignant spiritual. The spiritual was "Didn't My Lord Deliver Daniel?" It asked what was for me a hugely important question. In case the words aren't familiar, here is what the spiritual asks (this is a traditional spiritual and while the thrust is the same, specific words may vary).

Didn't my Lord deliver Daniel,

Deliver Daniel, deliver Daniel?

Didn't my Lord deliver Daniel?

Then why not every man?

He delivered Daniel from the lion's den,

And Jonah from the belly of the whale,

And the Hebrew children from the fiery flame,

Then why not every man?"

This seemed to me an earth-shaking question. Yes! If the Lord could deliver Daniel, then why not the slaves who toiled under the whip of the people who said they owned them? Why only take on Pharaoh? Where the heck was justice? Where was God?

These were important, pivotal questions. That said, again I have to own that it wasn't until it struck so close to home for me that I at last launched into my tirade, demanding answers from God, if indeed God was there—and I had growing doubts about that as well.

By the time I reached age 50, I had come to grips with what justice meant to me. I was one with the first two definitions of justice in the OED: moral uprightness and equity. For me the two went together. There could not be moral uprightness without equity. And there could be no equity without moral uprightness. In that regard, I was very much one with what the founders of the United States said. To be clear, I both agreed with what they *said* about equality and was hugely disappointed that they didn't follow through with their thoughts as I would have hoped.

From the *Declaration of Independence*: "We hold these truths to be self-evident, that all men are created equal, that they are endowed by their Creator with certain unalienable Rights, that among these are Life, Liberty and the pursuit of Happiness."

Unfortunately, the country became one where all men were *not* considered equal. Otherwise, it was such a profound and beautiful statement of the sanctity of justice.

From the preamble to the Constitution: "We the People of the United States, in Order to form a more perfect Union, establish Justice, ensure domestic Tranquility, provide for the common defense, promote the general Welfare, and secure the Blessings of Liberty to ourselves and our Posterity, do ordain and establish this Constitution of the United States of America."

It's worth noting that one of the first things out of the box is establishing justice. It's also worth noting that the Constitution was intended to secure the blessings of liberty for posterity, not just the founders. These things were brought home to me by a class in Constitutional Law for Non-Lawyers that I took, I think, in my late thirties. It was in that class that it was made clear that "equal protection under the law," as laid out in the Fourteenth Amendment, meant all of us, *all* of us, regardless of race, religion, or any other attempt at division.

It was clear to me, then, what justice meant, but it was just as clear that we lived in a hugely unjust world. So, what was God's role? If there was a God, which was something I struggled with, how could a loving God allow such injustice? These were the questions rising in my mind, heart, and soul in 1999.

I was supremely fortunate. I demanded answers and then actually got them. And several of these answers concerned justice.

CHAPTER ELEVEN

I'd like to share first what was perhaps the most stunning revelation regarding justice that was shared with me.

Separate the criminal from you, but lift not your hand against him except to defend yourself. Vengeance is Mine. Protect yourselves from harm, but seek not revenge. If you would love Me, love my creation.

There was a lot here to unpack. Indeed, there was more to unpack than I realized even the first ten or twelve times I read it. The implications for our system of justice, or what we call our system of justice, were profound.

"Separate the criminal from you." Ok, fine. That fit into what we call our criminal justice system. This was the role of the police, the district attorneys, and the judges: to determine who has violated our laws and then to separate the criminal from us. That said, the next part of the sentence is huge: "but lift not your hand against him except to defend yourself."

At first, I thought it referred to our police and how they handled themselves. "Lift not your hand against him except to defend yourself." Yes, that's how our police should act. But the more I thought about it, the more I realized this had less to do with policing and more to do with how we treat the convicted criminal. The implications seemed vast.

Most important, at least to me, this went to the very heart of our legal system. So often, many complain about a lawbreaker who "should have had" a harsher sentence. This statement makes clear and strips away any façade that hides from us that our justice system is about punishment and, perhaps but only a bit less clearly, revenge. Our legal system does have elements of rehabilitation. That should be warmly acknowledged and celebrated. Still, what we call our system of justice leans, and not just a little, toward retribution. We seek to get even.

I deeply believe we are called to help it lean strongly the other way, that our efforts and indeed our funding should be focused on how better to rehabilitate. This is the path to which our spiritual traditions call us.

A few beautiful examples (again, please see the wonderful books, *One Heart* and *World Scripture*) —

"The one who takes vengeance or bears a grudge acts like one who, having cut one hand while handling a knife, takes vengeance by stabbing the other hand." Jerusalem Talmud Nedarim 9.4

"Where there is forgiveness, there God dwells." Adi Granth (Sikhism)

"Then Peter came up and said to him, 'Lord, how often shall my brother sin against me, and I forgive him? As many as seven times?' Jesus said to him, 'I do not say to you seven times, but seventy times seven.'" Matthew 18:21-22

"If you are humble, and overlook and forgive, then Allah is forgiving and merciful" Qur'an 64:14

Jails and prisons, then, should not exist to dole out punishment. Their purpose is to separate the criminal from us. Yet, if jails and prisons should not be instruments of punishment and revenge, then what?

For me, the answer became clear. Justice doesn't end when the criminal is incarcerated. Indeed, that is only the beginning. If we are to separate the criminal from us but not seek revenge, then our jails and prisons should be constructed and run as places of rehabilitation. This means not simply funding for prisons, but major, not token. funding for education, counseling, and healthcare.

I believe that, for the most part, crime is a disease and we should treat it as such. We need, then, to use our prisons as hospitals of rehabilitation. As but one example, I have read that many in our prisons never finished school. I believe that needs to be addressed before they are released. Again and always, rehabilitation, not vengeance.

Over my lifetime, I'd heard people advocate for this, and I'd heard as well the angry reply that this would be pampering the criminals among us. I was introduced to the word *mollycoddle* (to treat with absurd indulgence). Was God now instructing us to mollycoddle the criminal? To answer that question immediately seemed to me just a reactionary response. To deal with it responsibly required some long and deep pondering.

This is what became clear to me after that pondering. There are indeed truly evil people in the world. To deny this is to be willfully blind. That said, it seemed and seems to me that most people who do bad or evil things are not irredeemably evil. All of our spiritual paths recognize this. It is why love and forgiveness are such integral parts of our spiritual traditions. If, then, we would integrate our legal system with what we hold to be our moral imperatives, we really do need to rethink things.

When a crime has its roots in evil, the criminal must indeed be separated from society. For me, that's what life sentences and life without possibility of parole are about. However, when a crime is the result of, as but one example, poverty, then we need not only to rehabilitate the criminal but also to address the poverty that bred the crime. We need to look at and consciously address the root causes of so much that results in criminal behavior. This is not a new thought, and the pushback against it is telling. "You're just excusing crime! You're giving the criminal a pass!" I don't think so.

As I pondered it, it became ever clearer to me that "justice" indeed means very different things to different people—as it has for decades, indeed millennia. That fact needs to be acknowledged and respected. It takes us back to "an eye for an eye," which is the "justice" not only of Exodus but the code of Hammurabi. Still, if we are to proclaim and embrace a loving moral code as our spiritual foundation, is "an eye for an eye" really who we want to be now, today, in this world?

Yet, if it's the word of God …

But is it? I think not.

"Vengeance is Mine." This is worth exploring more deeply. It would seem that God has claimed that privilege from the beginning—taking vengeance out of our human hands. In ancient times this was seen as showing God was vengeful. In ancient times, at least in what would become Judaism, God was indeed seen as jealous and angry, as well as vengeful, and needed to be placated. The call to fear that God, then, was certainly understandable. Even so, vengeance is reserved for God.

What about today? Should we still be fearing a jealous and vengeful God? I think not. Yet, God is still saying "Vengeance is Mine." What might this mean?

I do not believe it speaks of a vengeful God. I believe it is a reminder to humanity not to be vengeful. I see it as God saying, "If there's any vengeance that needs to be done, I'll do it. You should concentrate on loving one another." I see it also as God making clear that while "Vengeance is Mine," we are also being told, "And I choose not to take it. Let that be a lesson."

What? We are called to forgo revenge and rather to rehabilitate and (gasp) forgive? Yes. This has been the repeated call to humanity for centuries and seems yet another vegetable that we have carefully avoided. Which brings us to the most extreme penalty in our criminal justice system: the death penalty. It seems pretty clear to me that the death penalty is about vengeance, not justice.

Not justice? I have been asked by many how I can say that. A murderer, I'm told, should be put to death! How else can we show that life is sacred? Really? Let's think about that.

What this argument is saying is that life is so sacred that we are willing to kill to show just how sacred life is. That makes no sense. For me, a death penalty does not affirm that life is sacred. It denies that life is sacred. If life were sacred, we wouldn't take it.

Not to mention that try as we will to get it right, mistakes happen. If a person is found innocent after years in jail, it's horrific, but we can at last release that person. If a person is found innocent after being executed, there is nothing that can be done. It would seem to me that justice, our call to moral law, demands that no one be executed. The death penalty should be part of a past we have left behind, not a present that we embrace. Which takes us back to justice. If justice is not retribution and instead is observing moral law, what might that mean to us today, in this modern world?

For me, there can be no separation of justice from a moral code. And where does that leave God? This is a large part of what led me, after considerable thought, to understand God not as a puppet master pulling strings but as Cosmic Conscience calling us over and over again to this moral law, the law that Confucius found both true and hidden all those thousands of years ago.

"You can't legislate morality!" many have cried. They're right. They are indeed right. Morality cannot be legislated. Should we then simply forget morality? Should we abandon our commitment to a moral code, and, let's be honest, abandon the call of Cosmic Conscience that we live moral lives? It is indeed true that we cannot legislate people acting morally, but that doesn't mean we should relegate acting with moral purpose to the garbage bin.

A part of our moral code, a part that for me far too often is not carefully observed, is "equal justice under the law." If justice isn't equal, then it isn't justice. What impedes equal justice? Among so many things, I see racism and sexism as huge impediments to equal justice. I believe that if we are to be truly committed to moral law we must consciously and, as they are so strongly embedded in our culture, persistently work to eradicate these blights.

The time has come, then, to differentiate between our criminal code, which establishes what is legal and what is not, and our justice code, which establishes what is moral/ethical and what is not. Both are needed. We should never lose sight of that. Yet, the two are different, and we should not lose sight of that, either.

That said, I deeply believe that we need to bring dealing with crime and our moral code in harmony with one another. How do we do that? We bring them together by understanding and embracing that love and justice are one. Love cannot exist without justice. Justice cannot exist without love. This connection of love and justice is profound and important. It's definitely worth its own chapter.

CHAPTER TWELVE

The connection of love to justice was not something I had seen before the revelations. I had tried to live a just life. I had tried to live a loving life, but I'd never made a connection between these two efforts, which frankly I had seen as quite separate—important yes, but separate. Then came this.

Yours is not to judge! Yours is to love and help one another.

This made the connection a lot clearer and frankly caused some initial confusion. Not that I hadn't rebelled against the idea of sitting in judgment of others. I had, and strongly. When I was introduced to the words of Matthew 7:1, and to be honest this was long before I knew it was to be found in the Book of Matthew, my reaction was a resounding, "No, thank you!"

"Judge not, lest thou be judged" just didn't sit well. It seemed self-centered. Don't do something because it might happen to me? That's the only reason? It felt very much like saying that if something won't happen to me I shouldn't be concerned. I couldn't buy that. I was pre-teen, perhaps in my early teens, when I first read a line in a John Donne poem that went straight to my heart and stayed there: "Any man's death diminishes me, for I am one with mankind." Yes, I am one with mankind. This eternal truth meant that not only does any person's death diminish me, but also any person's hurt or hunger. I am one with mankind.

Here's another personal truth. I had long thrown off worrying what other people thought about me, good or bad. I disdained both praise and condemnation with equal lack of regard. It seemed to me that both spoke more about the person giving it than the person receiving it. Looking back, this was rather extreme and very much the result of my youth. Only in my later years did it sink in that there is such a thing as loving criticism, and that loving criticism should be listened to carefully. This doesn't mean that loving criticism is always correct! But it is worth listening to. For me, loving criticism is by its very nature not judgmental. Still, what mattered to me in my youth and still matters today is not what other people think about me but whether I can respect the person staring back at me in the mirror every morning when I wash.

In terms of justice, I rewrote Matthew. For me it was, "Judge not, lest thou be wrong!" We humans are fallible creatures, and I'm human. I cannot possibly know enough about another person's life experiences, and most particularly the how and why that person acts or has acted, to sit in judgment of anyone.

Many years later, I found this wonderful quote from Sufi Islam: "Happy are those who find fault with themselves instead of finding fault with others." Yes! Said much better and far more clearly than I had phrased it and so many, many years earlier.

How, then, does "Yours is not to judge! Yours is to love and help one another" fit with our system of "justice"? I believe it fits in a crucially important way that I hadn't understood before. As the revelation from the previous chapter made clear, we should indeed separate the criminal from us. We need to stay safe. That's important! Being safe is not an idle consideration, but what we are being told is not to focus only there. In separating the criminal from us, we should not seek vengeance. Justice demands love, not vengeance.

Thus, our criminal "justice" system should exist to keep us safe and at the same time *not* indulge in extracting vengeance. Our judges are, then, not administering justice: they are holding people accountable for crimes, if guilty, and acting to separate the criminal from us to keep us safe if this is necessary. This is significant! To get there required a lot of thought on my part and, frankly, a rethinking of courts and judges and justice.

Justice, then, lies in our hearts and our actions, not in our courts. Our courts determine what is legal and, one hopes, what is not. This in no way means that justice lacks importance. Indeed, it is critically important. What it does mean is that we should look for *accountability* in our legal system. True *justice* lies elsewhere. Of course, I'm hardly the first person to see this.

Consider the murders of so many Black people by White people whose racism brought them to commit murder. At last, in so many cases at *long* last, some of the racist murderers have been tried and found guilty. Many in the Black community have proclaimed loudly that justice was *not* done simply by finding the people guilty. They are right. These murderers were held accountable, and that is certainly a welcome and positive step. But justice requires that we deal with racism, not just the racist, that we hold accountable not only those whose racism brings them to violent acts but also those who maliciously provide them with fodder to feed that racism. So again, justice lies not in our courts but in our hearts, minds, and souls. Justice involves what we do.

What, then, should we do?

Open your hearts to those in need. Think ye that I cannot see? Think ye a phrase muttered in church or mosque or synagogue can hide from Me the truth of your heart?

As with so many of the revelations, there's a lot to unpack here. The clearest, most obvious aspect is the charge to open our hearts to those in need. This charge is clear and very often repeated throughout history as well as very often ignored. We need to be helping our brothers and sisters in need. What spiritual tradition would disagree with that? But there's more than that here.

"Think ye that I cannot see? Think ye a phrase muttered in church or mosque or synagogue can hid from Me the truth of your heart?" This nails it. We have paid superficial commitment to the poor within our communities, it would seem, since the beginning of time. Rabbis, ministers, priests, and imams (and others) preach about it. We sing about it, talk about it, and then do so very little—much too often congratulating ourselves on the little we actually do. And here is Cosmic Conscience calling us on it. What is important, we are told, is not what comes pouring out of our mouths, but our hearts. What is important is that we *do* that which we talk so much about. And we cannot "do" without the active involvement of our hearts. Yet again, justice and love are inextricably intertwined.

For a while, that's where I stopped. There was certainly plenty to think about! But there was another implication that began to take hold which for me made even more solid my belief in God as Cosmic Conscience. If we will listen, God can provide us guidance. If we are open, God can point us to the moral path. But what God cannot do is walk that path for us! This was worth a lot of time and thought.

I have come to believe that Cosmic Conscience very much hopes to guide us, indeed wants to guide us. To do so, Cosmic Conscience will reach out to us, if we are truly wanting to listen and open to hearing. I'm living proof of that as have been so many people before me. And if Cosmic Conscience will reach out and touch *me*, then *all* of us are capable of being touched. What is required of us is an open heart as well as open ears. Clearly the call of Cosmic Conscience isn't new, but, with luck, perhaps this time more of us will listen.

I believe that we live in a truly challenging time. We need only look about ourselves to see that. Cosmic Conscience is urging us to be moral, indeed hopes that we will in fact act righteously and walk the ethical, moral path that is available to us, all of us, IF we are willing.

But by God telling us that the truth of hearts is known and will not be mitigated by prayer, or sermon, or song, God is also telling us that what will happen depends not on God's will, but ours. God does not create good or evil. We do. God does not physically interfere in human history, which is why it is not our prayers that matter but the action or inaction prompted by our hearts. God is there, whispering in our ear, if we will listen, about love and justice and how we might help each other as fellow creatures on the planet we call Earth.

"Yours is to love and help one another."

There is no justice without love nor love without justice. Humanity has tried to separate the two for millennia, causing untold pain and humiliation for our human family. Without justice *and* love, community is not possible, and without community, peace is not possible.

What this requires of us, I believe, is a full-on commitment to community. Despite all of the divisions we seek to fashion, division by race, religion, ethnicity, sex, or wealth, we are one family, and we need not only to remember that but also to act upon it.

This above all. For so long as you put yourself before others, so long will you lose yourself and your way and increase the distance between us.

Which brings us to the next section: "The Call to Community."

Part Five:
The Call to Community

CHAPTER THIRTEEN

If there is anything that is as common within our diverse spiritual traditions as the call to love one another, and just as commonly ignored, it is the call to oneness, to community. It makes sense. The more I thought about it, the more I realized that community and love are linked (as in "Do unto others …"). Indeed, I believe that community, love, and justice are all linked. It finally dawned on me that if we violate or ignore one, we've in fact ignored them all. This is what all of our spiritual traditions have been *trying* for so long to pound into our unwilling hearts and minds. I realize, then, that the two crucial revelations I received about community are nothing new. Nor are they submitted as new. But they do indeed bear repeating, ever more emphatically, to a human family that seems to need it spelled out, over and over again.

Think ye I prize green eyes over blue? Brown hair over blond? How can you say I would favor one gender over the other or hold one race as special unto Me and in the same breath pretend you love Me? To hate my creation is to hate Me. To despise My creation is to despise Me.

This is a universal call. Throughout this book I have found inspiration and confirmation in two books I keep mentioning, *One Heart* and *World Scripture*. The quotes below are all from *World Scripture*, and they reinforce the teachings from Judaism and Christianity we are so very familiar with.

"Let all mankind be thy sect." Adi Granth, Japuji 28 (Sikh)

"Let us have concord with our own people, and concord with people who are strangers to us." Atharva Veda 7.52 (Hindu)

"When one finger is sore, you do not cut it off." Nigerian proverb (Njak)

"All ye under heaven! Regard heaven as your father, earth as your mother, and all things as your brothers and sisters." Oracle of Atsuta (Shinto)

"So what of all these titles, names, and races? They are mere worldly conventions." Suta Nipata 648 (Buddhism)

"O contending peoples and kindreds of the earth! Set your faces toward unity, and let the radiance of its light shine upon you." Gleanings from Bahaullah 111 (Baha'i)

"O mankind! We created you from a single pair of male and female and made you into nations and tribes, that you might know each other." Qur'an 49.13 (Islam)

This is, of course, just a taste. We are different; this is acknowledged. But we are called to respect and indeed enjoy those differences. As the Qur'an puts it, we should use our diversity to get to know each other better, *not* to fight amongst ourselves! Or, as was spelled out in another of the revelations granted me:

Lift a hand against another, and you lift your hand against Me.

Could this possibly be any clearer? Yet, over and over again, century after century, we have divided ourselves. If there was ever an unending human quest, it would appear to be to seek out new ways for us to divide. We divide over what we call race. We divide over our spiritual traditions. We divide over ethnicity. We divide over nations. Nor does it stop there. We divide over cities (*my* city is better than *yours*!). We divide over states. We divide over language. We divide over sports teams (and get into arguments and even fights over our teams, as well as take pride in "our" team while demeaning someone else's).

Our search for division seems endless. Yet through it all, we are called on repeatedly not to divide ourselves but to embrace community. The sad, repeated truth is that all too often, even when we embrace the call to community in our rhetoric, we reject it in how we act. So let's step back a moment. A call to community? Really?

To be clear, to embrace community is not to assert that we are all the same. We aren't! As those of us who come from large families will agree, members of the same family are all separate human beings, differing in size, in temperament, and in beliefs. The call to community is a call to revel in as well as respect our diversity, not to deny it. It is a call to embrace that diverse as we are, we are one family, the human family.

When we see a field filled with differing flowers and other assorted gifts of nature, let us enjoy and appreciate the flowers rather than spend our time and effort in the pointless task of trying to determine which flower is somehow best. The truth of it is, one flower might make a wonderfully tasty tea another a splendid herb seasoning, and another a glorious perfume, while yet another seems useless to humans but does a grand job of feeding birds—not to mention the vast assortment of colors, shapes, and sizes of the differing petals as they bloom. Any attempt to decide which flower is best becomes an absurd and irrelevant quest.

I believe that abandoning this quest for "best" is what our spiritual traditions have been begging of us. There is nothing to be gained and no point in ignoring our differences. They are real, but let us learn to enjoy and learn from these differences rather than fear them. Simple. Right? So, why do we remain deaf to this universal call, and what has that concerted deafness cost us?

Some of the costs are horrifically obvious. One of the most horrifying is that human history has been a history of war after war, only intermittently interrupted with brief interludes of peace. The lives lost and destroyed are truly immeasurable. Yet, throughout history, we have chosen war over community. With more and more nations again developing nuclear weapons, we threaten the very survival of the human family. Yet still, we chose war.

As if war weren't enough, today there is yet another threat to the very survival of humanity if we will not choose community. It is the global threat to the environment, the very Earth that is our home.

You have made my creation a sewer and worshipped wealth. Your greed condemns you.

I was gifted this revelation in 1999. At that time, I was very much aware of the erosion of our environment and the need to protect it. I'd read and appreciated Rachel Carson's *Silent Spring* and been energized by it. Yet, I had not yet heard of global warming or climate change. A little research tells me that some folks had been talking about these things for nearly a decade by then. Still, I only became aware of them in 2006, when Al Gore's book and documentary *An Inconvenient Truth* saw light. It was then that I fully realized how stark and important the above revelation was. Note that the revelation doesn't speak of a lack of a "right ritual" or "a plague of blasphemous talk." It's what we *do* (or don't do) that condemns us, not what we say. We have indeed made the Earth a sewer. The sad truth of it is that the Earth is still a sewer. Far too many still love, indeed worship, wealth far more than community. We think of holding onto our gain in the now with little regard for the loss that those who follow us (including our children who are just now growing up) will endure.

To this day, those who would try to clean up the sewer we humans have made of our Earth struggle with those who value wealth and power far more highly than posterity. For far too many, acting responsibly is just "too expensive." "Me, me, me! I have to take care of *me*!" they shout, with little or no thought to the community of "us."

Greed, then, does indeed condemn us. It not only condemns our planet to remaining a sewer, but also condemns us to a changing climate that ensures that life will only get worse, a lot worse for humanity and all life on the planet. Still, greed is but one facet of our repeated commitment to "me, me, me" that flies so completely in the face of our spiritual calling to think of community and not simply ourselves.

Why?! Why has community proved to be so difficult for us?

I believe there are a number of reasons for our continuing rejection of community, and we'll discuss at least a few of them in the next chapter. For now, I would like to close this chapter with a clarion call and a warning. One compelling reason we have remained deaf to the call of community is that our willingness to be divided helps to make us pliable, insecure, and deeply afraid. Our search for "which flower is best" has left our lives open to manipulation and our souls free to be plundered.

Many have grabbed hold of this "opportunity." Encouraging, indeed feeding our fears has been for many a welcome path both to power and wealth. We need to remember that the person who tells us to "fear" those who are "different" seeks to enslave us. And for centuries, they've been incredibly successful slave masters.

If we would be whole and free, we must shun those who would divide us. We must never forget that the person who tells us to be fearful seeks to own us. We must send fear of diversity and those who preach it packing. Let's explore this as well as other barriers to community.

CHAPTER FOURTEEN

My children are my children, and I love them all. How dare you think I would choose between them!

We cannot possibly list in one book, let alone a single chapter, all of the obstacles to community we have so resolutely created for ourselves. That said, I would like to explore the three that leapt out to me as I studied the revelations and asked myself, "Why is this so hard? Why is it that we have throughout history and continue to this day to assert that God chooses between us?" The three obstacles (out of so many possible candidates) that I want to examine are fear of "other," greed/the need to acquire, and arrogance/Me, Me, Me. What intrigued me, as I studied them, is that they are so inter-related. In fact, there's really no discussing one without discussing the other two. That said, let's try to deal with them somewhat separately at least at first.

It seems clear that the most fundamental obstacle to community throughout the centuries has been fear. We humans are nothing if not fearful. We know how completely fear has controlled us by the sheer number of times in Hebrew and then Christian scripture God exhorts us to turn away from fear. One example (out of hundreds!) may be found in the very first book of Torah. In Genesis (15.1) God tells Abraham, "Be not afraid." Then, after "Be not afraid is repeated over and over in Hebrew scripture, it is repeated yet again in Christian scripture. As but one example, there's Acts (18.9) when God tells Paul, "Be not afraid."

Why do we need to be told over and over to "Be not afraid"? It's because we have been and remain a fear-filled species. We fear so much that it would be pointless to try to chronicle or enumerate all of what we fear. For us here, the great fear to speak of, the fear that has rendered community all but impossible in our lives, is our raging fear of "other"—other races, other religions, other ethnicities. "Those people." We fear "those people." What they might do. What they might not do. What they might think. What they might not think. What they might say. What they might not say. Not that our spiritual traditions haven't repeatedly tried to warn us about disunity and fearing "other."

"My children, war, fear, and disunity have brought you from your villages to this sacred council fire. Facing a common danger, and fearing for the lives of your families, you have yet drifted apart, each tribe thinking and acting only for itself." Hiawatha, Onodaga tradition

"Every kingdom divided against itself is laid waste, and no city or house divided against itself will stand." Matthew 12.25

"The pebbles are the strength of the wall." Buji proverb (Africa)

"The problem with clinging to a single doctrine is that it plunders the Way." Mencius VII.A.26 (Confucianism)

"To be attached to a certain view and to look down upon others' views as inferior—this the wise call a fetter." Sutta Nipata 798 (Buddhism)

Still, we cling ferociously to our divisions. Fear of "other" destroys our confidence, cripples our compassion, and consigns our ability to think to the dustbin. If we would be free, we must break the bonds of this fear. For me, a first step in breaking our bonds is understanding just how tightly twined about us the chains of fear truly are. And again, primary among the fears that plague us is the crippling fear of "other."

I believe a large part of why we fear "other" is that we are so very afraid of being less than "other." We fear "other" because we fear being weaker. We fear "other" because our own ability to hold onto any real meaning to our lives is so tenuous that we are afraid that if the "other" has meaning, we will lose ours.

I believe it important to understand that one major reason our fears remain so strong is because, scriptural admonishments notwithstanding, what has brought so many so much power and wealth over the centuries is encouraging, even feeding our fears. In truth, exploiting fear is quite possibly the most lucrative occupation there is. And this is in no way confined to politics. Many a fortune has been made marketing a product that plays to our insecurities and fears.

Beyond that, encouraging and indeed preaching fear is a favored tool of the demagogue. In contrast, community is the demagogue's great enemy. We fear "other." What the demagogue fears is the unity birthed by community. That fear of unity is what prompts the demagogue to do any and everything possible to divide us. "Divide and diminish" is the pathway for many to wealth. "Divide and conquer" is the pathway for the would-be demagogue. Beyond that, I would submit that "Subdivide and rule" is how the demagogue stays in power. In a spiritual sense, the secret to attaining and then keeping power over a people is to deprive them of any real sense of meaning to their lives—and then put yourself forward as the one person, holding the one "right belief," who can help them regain what they fear they have lost.

As but one example, let us look at White supremacy and why it is so strongly preached by one group and embraced by another. There are those who preach White supremacy to gain, hold, and enforce both their grip on power and the size of their bank account. There is a second group that clings to the hope of White supremacy because they have lost any real belief in themselves and their value as members of the human family. They believe they are so small, so insignificant that if they lose the "supremacy" of their Whiteness, they will vanish. They are, therefore, understandably ferocious in their defense of Whiteness. And with that defense comes a wall that renders human community all but impossible. The cry "I have to be better than *somebody*" still rings in my ears.

This is but one example of the toxicity of fear. Much too often we fear people who practice a spiritual tradition differing from our own. We fear people whose ethnicity is different from our own. There is and can be no single reason for the fears that paralyze us. I would offer not "the" reason for our fears but what I believe is one other reason. We have accepted the idea that there is only so much room on the metaphorical ladder that can lead us to a better life—both more meaningful and more comfortable. If there is only "so much" room on the ladder, and if someone else is climbing up, then there's no room for me! I need to pull others off the ladder so I have room. I have to look out for me.

Which brings us to what I believe is so often a fear-induced sense of arrogance: "Me, Me, Me!" How do we know we have a problem with our "Me, Me, Me" mentality? We know because over the centuries all of our spiritual traditions have been reminding us, pleading with us over and over again to set aside arrogance. Setting aside pride is yet another of the vegetables that we humans like to ignore. Most of the examples below are from *One Heart*.

"Pride goeth before destruction, and a haughty spirit before a fall." Proverbs 16.18 (Judaism)

"Give up anger; renounce pride; transcend all worldly attachments." Dhammapada 221 (Buddhism)

"Let your gait be modest and your voice low: the most hideous of voices is the braying of the ass." Qur'an 31.19 (Islam)

"The humane are high-minded, not proud: the vulgar are proud, but not high-minded." Analects 13.26 (Confucianism)

"Those who try to outshine others dim their own light. Those who boast of their accomplishments diminish the things they have done." Tao Te Ching 24 (Taoism)

"Shun all pride and jealousy." Bhagavata Purana 11.4 (Hinduism)

Our spiritual traditions would not have to keep reminding us to be humble if it weren't for the unfortunate fact that we keep forgetting. Far too often, we make up our minds, make our decisions, and then act with the comfortable belief in the supremacy of "Me." You take care of you. I look after me. For me, "*I* come first. *I'm* the one who is important." With this as a framework, community becomes impossible. If we are always "looking out for number one," everyone else, by definition, becomes at best secondary. We are left with only self-centered individuals seeking what seems best for them without regard to what may hurt or degrade others.

We must somehow find a way to move beyond "Me." As Bahaullah so eloquently put it:

"Beware, lest ye prefer yourselves above your neighbors." Gleanings from the writings of Bahaullah 146.1 (Baha'i)

I believe arrogance, and feelings of irrelevance that are accompanied by belief in the lack of a meaningful life are quite often two sides to the same, exceedingly unfortunate coin. Both play a role in sabotaging our quest for community. It's essential, therefore, to understand that moving past our fixation with "me" does *not* mean embracing that we are unimportant as individuals! We are important. It is *not* a question of either/or. What it does mean is that if our interest stops at ourselves we have defeated our attempt at community.

As Rabbi Hillel so ably put it:

"If I am not for myself, who will be for me? Yet if I am only for myself, what am I?" (Pirkei Avot 1:14)

What are we if we are only for ourselves? Arrogant.

Which brings us to a separate but deeply related side of our pridefully arrogant "Me, Me, Me." Greed. Our cultures have taught us that we can never have enough. Whatever we have, we want more. We "need" more. Century after century, our diverse cultures have taught us this even as our spiritual traditions, century after century they have warned us against it. Greed, by its very nature, becomes a huge roadblock to any sense of community. Again, from *World Scripture* and *One Heart*:

"What is that love which is based on greed? When there is greed, the love is false." Adi Granth, Shalok, Farid p. 1378 (Sikhism)

"He who loves money will not be satisfied with money; nor he who loves wealth, with gain: this also is vanity." Ecclesiastes 5.10 (Judaism)

"The love of money is the root of all evils." 1 Timothy 6.10 (Christianity)

"Those who preserve themselves from their own greed will surely prosper." Qur'an 59.9 (Islam)

"O my wealth-coveting and foolish soul, when will you succeed in emancipating yourself from the desire for wealth?" Mahabharata, Santiparva 177.25 (Hinduism)

For me, the most succinct and in-our-face pronouncement comes from Confucianism, through the sage Mencius, writing some 2,300 years ago! "If you cultivate wealth, you give up humanity. If you cultivate humanity, you give up wealth." (III.A.3)

I believe that it's worth noting that wealth itself is not a barrier to community. 1 Timothy is often misquoted. It is not money that is the root of evil, it is the *love* of money. One who has wealth can indeed use that wealth to promote community. It is the love of wealth, the pursuit of wealth, the putting of wealth at the forefront of our lives that blinds us to the worth and needs of others and keeps us from the community to which our spiritual paths have called us.

I believe that fear is often the driving factor behind both arrogance and greed. We humans are so fearfully insecure (an insecurity continually fed by those who would profit by it) that we puff out our chests with pride to cover the fact that in truth we think so little of ourselves. I believe we are tempted to grasp at wealth because we see so little value in who we are that we hope to attain value in what we own. This doesn't simply keep us from community, it actively drives us away from it.

Of course, and I trust obviously, there are numerous other substantial and exceedingly important drawbacks to allowing greed, arrogance, and fear to govern our lives. While by no means minimizing how much they degrade our lives and our humanity, here we are only focusing on one: how they have impacted and indeed thwarted attempts at reaching community both throughout history and today—a time when we so desperately need to come together as the human family.

So, is community forever out of our grasp? Is there nothing that we can do to achieve it? In the next chapter we'll explore some possible answers and one answer in particular that I believe may help us in our quest for community. *Not* that we will be searching for, let alone find, "the one true" answer! Rather, perhaps we may find a few answers that will at least point us in a positive direction.

CHAPTER FIFTEEN

Imagine community. True community. Imagine coming together as one people, warmly respecting, valuing, and enjoying the diversity of our human family as we respect, value, and warmly enjoy knowing that each and every one of us is a unique and special human being. In truth, some of us may find this undesirable or even threatening. For most of us, however, I believe we recognize that this is what we've been called to for millennia.

As we explore some possible paths to community, it's important to realize that a sure path to destroying community, as it is a sure path to destroying all of our spiritual quests, is to search for "the one right answer." We do indeed need to search for answers! That's not at issue. But our search should never be with blinders on, with one favored answer in sight and to the exclusion of any who might see a differing path.

I deeply believe that a search for "the" answer to our spiritual conundrums invites us to embrace zealotry. This is the chosen path of tyrants and demagogues, as they claim possession of the one and only answer and gladly punish any who would disagree. Throughout history, this arrogant path has repeatedly crippled all of our spiritual traditions. So, in exploring a few paths, and one path in particular for embracing community, it's important not to see or embrace it as the "only" path. That said, I believe one crucial path to our goal of community is the path of humility.

I'm reminded of a favorite play, *Inherit the Wind*. It's a fictionalized dramatization of the Scopes trial, when a teacher is put on trial for teaching Darwin in his schoolroom. At the end of the film version, Spencer Tracy, who plays the attorney for the defense, slaps together his copies of both Darwin and Holy Scripture. Holding them in his hand he says, "The Bible is a book. It's a good book, but it's not the only book." What a life lesson ... if we are open to learning it!

That said, after contemplating for years both the need for community and the roadblocks humanity has placed on our path to reach it, my search for a viable path brought me back yet again to the Prophet Micah. "What does the Lord require of you? Only this: to act with justice, love compassion, and to walk humbly with your God." Micah didn't point out where this path would lead, and I didn't see it clearly for years. But what is it that we get if we will act with justice, love compassion, and walk humbly? We get a real and thriving sense of community. We get the peace that we are called to and strive for. We get a validation of our own worth as well as and at the same moment, the worth of our entire human family. We gain the spiritual fulfilment and renewal we so deeply long for and that our spiritual traditions keep holding out in front of us. Powerful stuff!

After years of study, I at last came to realize that love, justice, and humility not only intersect in community, they are exactly what makes community possible. Having spent considerable time exploring love and justice in earlier chapters, the time has come to examine humility.

First, and perhaps most important, we need to agree upon what is meant here by humility. Some see humility as putting ourselves down. If we are humble, it's because we don't believe in ourselves and our worth. I don't believe that for a moment. And it's certainly *not* what we'll be talking about here. Nor, for that matter, do I for a moment believe that it's what Micah was talking about. Humility is *not* saying I am nothing. Humility is saying that I'm a valuable human being—but no more valuable than are all my brothers and sisters.

For me, then, humility has nothing to do with thinking less of ourselves. Rather, it is recognizing and embracing the inherent worthiness both of ourselves *and* all our brothers and sisters. This is crucial. Embracing humility teaches us that our value as a human being is not made greater by our wealth, nor is it lessened by a lack of wealth. Our value as a human being is not made greater by our fame, nor is it lessened by a lack of fame. It is not made greater by our race, ethnicity, or spiritual tradition, nor is it lessened by our race, ethnicity, or spiritual tradition. Humility is the great equalizer. It is recognizing that our diversity is like the diversity of flowers in the field. Community is recognizing and acknowledging that different as we are, we all grow in that same field.

In his prose poem "Desiderata," Max Ehrmann writes, "You are a child of the universe, no less than the trees and the stars; you have a right to be here." These are important, empowering words. Humility acknowledges this and at the same moment acknowledges that this is true of every person. We are *all* children of the universe. We are, *all* of us, no less than the trees and the stars. And we *all* have a right to be here. This is huge.

Humility embraced and lived is empowering. Indeed, we might call it that: empowered humility.

Not to say that humility comes naturally in a culture that so widely disparages it. Despite repeated calls from our spiritual traditions, we are bombarded daily by claims that attach humility to shame. In our divided world, we are told to be proud of ourselves, but I would strongly submit that, counter-cultural as it may seem, pride, and particularly a boisterous pride, finds its genesis in a feeling of insecurity and lack of self-worth. Pride is, then, a sign of weakness, not strength. This is the pride that all of our traditions warn us against. It is the people who must continually broadcast how important they are, how wealthy they are, how much "better" they are than others, who deep at their core believe their lives to be unimportant and without meaning. It is the humble, secure in their own self-worth, who are able to respect others and not feel that their own fragile sense of self requires them to put others down.

So, I believe one of the most important steps to embracing community is embracing a healthy sense of humility. Given where humanity is at this moment, this will not come easily. We should recognize that. It will take time and intention. That said, humility is such a valuable goal that I would urge us to have more than just the intention. Let us commit to the goal of humility and then to working tirelessly toward that goal. This can help us at long last to have the strength we need to fulfill our call to community.

What, then, is the strength of humility? If, as Micah urges, we walk humbly with our God, then we can be respectful of people whose experience of God or no God is different from our own and not feel threatened by their differing beliefs.

Humility allows us to be comfortable enough, secure enough of ourselves and who we are, that that when faced (as we are daily) with people whose race, ethnicity, cultural background, and yes, religion differs from ours, we can enjoy our differences and not feel threatened by them. I believe humility is the very bedrock of community. In truth, both puffed-up arrogance and feelings of inferiority as well as fear play equal roles in sabotaging community.

Again and most emphatically, healthy humility does not equate with feeling inadequate or worthless. We need to recognize and teach this to ourselves and our children. Timidity is not humility. Lack of self-worth is not humility. Feeling shame is not humility. Indeed, I believe there is no way to approach life humbly unless we feel secure that the person we are has meaning, that we truly are no less than the trees and the stars and have a right, an irrevocable right to be here! It is a lack of humility that allows and sometimes causes us to lash out at others. It is long past time to recognize that humbly embracing our common humanity both empowers and frees us.

Frees us? From what? This is crucial. Humility does *not* free us from fear. It frees us from becoming debilitated by fear—most especially, the fear of "other." It frees us as well from the oppressive arrogance of "Me, Me, Me." And it frees us from a call to greed.

How?

I believe the best key we have to unlock the chains that keep us enslaved by the fear of "other" as well as other debilitating fears is humility. It's worth repeating that humility can not and does not free us from fear. To be fearless is not the goal. What humility does is allow us to live with rather than be enslaved by what we fear. When we seek community, then, what we seek is not to be ruled by our fears, particularly but not solely the fear of "other."

Another benefit? A humble people do not see themselves as somehow "better" than others. Therefore, the fear of losing stature vanishes! A humble people do not see themselves as knowing everything. Therefore, the fear of admitting we don't have all the answers vanishes! Humility does not restrict us! It can free us, inspire us, and indeed ennoble us. Humility helps us to embrace that we all have value. We acknowledge we all have value, as well as acknowledging that neither wealth nor power, neither race nor ethnicity, can add or subtract to that value. Humility frees us to act in the world freed from worry about how others may see us.

Indeed, humility frees us from a fear of failure. The only requirement an engaged person of humility has is to do their best—with no value judgement as where their best lands in the grand scheme of things. The only potential failure that we as a humble people need be concerned with is did we fail to do the best we could without comparison to anyone else.

In *The Gondoliers*, Gilbert and Sullivan make fun of those who can't grasp humility. The Grand Inquisitor states, "When everybody's somebody, then no one's anybody." Not true. Our spiritual health does not depend on being "better than somebody." Our spiritual traditions have tried and keep trying to help us see that what we are called to is to *help* one another, not try to be better than one another. We are called to *love* one another, not divide ourselves and despise one another. If we will be humble, a truly wonder-filled world awaits us. So much to do and nothing to prove! Now that is truly empowering.

How might we get there? Step one is indeed to recognize that we all have value: wealthy and poor, well-educated and lacking education, whatever our race, religion, ethnicity, sexual orientation, we need to remember "You are a child of the universe … you have a right to be here." Will this by itself solve our problems? Of course not. But it's a start. It's a good step in a good direction. It moves us closer to the community our spiritual traditions have asked of us. And any journey we would take begins with that first step.

But, really, what's so great about community? Imagine this. Let's say we live in small, isolated town. There's no fire department. There are no hydrants and no hoses. But there is a river nearby. Suppose my house catches fire, and everyone around me thinks, "Well, it's not my house. Why should I get involved?" If that happens, my home will burn to the ground. Even if I survive the fire, I'll be homeless.

But what if everyone helps? What if those with one bucket run down to the river, those with more than one bring all the buckets they have, and those who have no buckets run down to river anyway to do what they can? What if folks form a bucket brigade from the river to my house and hand buckets full of water to one another and the folks at the end of the line, where my house is burning, throw water on the fire, while still others then run with empty buckets back down to the river to be re-filled? The truth of it is, it's still possible that despite everyone's best efforts the house will burn down. But what's more likely is that the fire will be put out and I'll still have a home. Why? Community action. We came together as a community. This time it was my house. Next time it might be yours. And it's always possible that we won't know the people who live in a house that catches fire. Still, we're a community, and when a house catches fire, regardless of whose house it is, we form a bucket brigade.

The simple lesson of it is this. No one person, even with a large bucket, could possibly extinguish the fire alone. And every person, down to a person with a small bucket or even no bucket at all, can play a part in putting the fire out. This is the essence of community.

So. how do we apply this? How do we take it out of simple story, apply to our so very complex world, and work to achieve spiritual community?

First, I believe it's helpful to realize that all we've been talking about throughout this book are truly differing aspects of the same whole. If we act with justice and embrace compassion, humility will follow. It must follow. If we would act with justice, we need to embrace love and humility. If we would embrace love, we need to act with justice and walk this Earth of ours with humility. The more I've lived with the revelations and thought about them, the clearer it has become to me that love, justice, and humility are not separate. Together, indeed only together, they bring us to community. It was when I at last grasped this that the whole of the revelations became understandable to me. They were not separate dictums, delivered by Cosmic Conscience as a "system dump." They were and are all related, all part of the same whole. And while I know I've been hugely imperfect in relating it, I hope the truth of this has shone through.

So, again, how do we apply this and work to achieve spiritual community? One way, not the only way but a strong, positive way, is by embracing Interfaith as a faith even as we walk our diverse spiritual paths. Indeed, Interfaith does not ask us to leave our spiritual traditions behind. What Interfaith does ask is that we walk our diverse spiritual paths with humility, both respecting and indeed learning from the paths that our brother and sisters walk, always realizing that it is not the path we walk but how we walk our path that counts. Let us get to the mountaintop where love, compassion, justice, and community humbly dwell. And let us celebrate the differing paths of all who are walking there. If we can embrace our diversity without fear or prejudice, if we can leave greed and arrogance behind us and walk this amazing planet with humility, we may yet reach true community.

If we are to rebuild our world, let us do it as family.

Part Six:
Some Conundrums Regarding the Divine

CHAPTER SIXTEEN

In this final section, we reach what is for me perhaps the most difficult topic to engage. Not that there haven't been discussions so far that folks of goodwill might well disagree with and see differently. In fact, I feel certain that there are. Still, it has always seemed to me that when we get specific talking about the divine, we can provoke some especially emotionally charged reactions. So, before proceeding with these chapters, a few things that I would hope to make clear.

First, there is a definite and important difference, at least to me, between belief and knowledge. So much of how we think about God or no God has to do with our beliefs. As an Interfaither, a person whose faith is Interfaith, I hold close that these differing beliefs should be respected and taken seriously. That said, I don't believe any of us can know. As an agnostic, I freely admit that while I don't know I *do* have beliefs. Many of these have become strong beliefs based on my experience and interaction with Cosmic Conscience. My beliefs, then, aren't in any way wishy-washy or whims, but understanding that while I believe, I do not know, helps me to respect and indeed listen with interest to people whose closely held beliefs may differ from mine.

With regards to the revelations I received, what I know is that I received them. What I know is that I was told to take dictation, heard the words in my head to get a pen and paper and write the revelations down. What I know is that these revelations addressed major questions in my life, including the questions of "Is there a God?" and "If God does indeed exist, what is the nature of God?"

I believe these revelations flowed from God. That said, there is no way to "know." Moreover, my beliefs cannot and do not explain the nature of God. Nor do they come anywhere near explaining the mystery of God that has been such a crucial part of human experience from our beginnings. One loving friend, who does not believe in God, explained the revelations as the overtime work of my own subconscious.

I don't believe that. Not for a moment. Still, I didn't argue for I cannot know. And while I deeply hold that we should be open to listening to one another and sharing our beliefs, I see nothing helpful in arguing about them. So again, the call to seek truth in what our varying spiritual traditions have in common made and makes sense to me. Moreover, the process of dealing with and living with these calls of the divine that we have in common, to my mind, may help us to a better understanding of God.

In this section, I'll be sharing some undoubtedly controversial beliefs. I believe them and take them seriously or I would not inflict them on you. But they are beliefs, not knowledge, and should be understood as such.

The particular belief I'd like to address in this chapter is my belief in God. I would not argue with any person of goodwill who does not believe in God. I would not argue with any person of goodwill who believes in God but believes differently than I. That said, this is the what and why of my belief in God.

As mentioned before, at the time I received the revelations, I was struggling deeply with the question of whether or not God existed. I had grown up having some doubts while still believing in a God of love and justice. Yet, there was so much hate and injustice in the world. Indeed, it seemed to be flourishing! If God existed, how could God allow this? There was as well the constant reference to God as He. Somehow, I popped out of the womb a male who believed in women as co-equal partners in our humanity. The "maleness" in Judaism and throughout so many differing spiritual traditions, at best disquieted and frequently angered me. To be clear, I never thought of women as superior to men. I thought of men and women as human, equally strong as well as weak, equally smart as well as dumb. This idea of God as male was offensive to me. I didn't buy it. Yet if there were a God, and if God were neither male nor female, then how could God have allowed patriarchy to run roughshod over our spiritual traditions for so long?

For me, the revelations answered those questions though it took living with them and pondering them to fully digest it. Perhaps the most difficult revelation to understand and come to grips with was this one:

That which breathes has a soul. Think ye you understand the space wherein I live? Your universe fills not my fist ... nor I it."

Say what? Some of what this offered seemed to make sense, and over the months and years of contemplating it I was able to integrate it into my beliefs. God was everywhere. Okay. God could not and should not be put into a small box of beliefs. Okay. That second aspect helped me in my path to Interfaith. We shouldn't be trying to shove God into a box, however convenient that might be. Our varying spiritual traditions needed to be thought as interpretations of the same God, not conflicting "right beliefs" as to God's nature. This helped me to integrate "Think ye you understand the space wherein I live?"

Still, "Your universe fills not my fist ... nor I it."?? This remained a puzzle for me until I interned at the Interfaith Community Church (now Interfaith Community Sanctuary) and shared ministry there with Imam Jamal Rahman (as well as Rev. Karen Lindquist and Rev. Debra Lajimodiere, two other beautiful souls), who quickly became my friend as well as brother. I preached on the fourth Sunday of the month. Jamal preached on a different Sunday. I was sitting with the congregation during one of Jamal's Sundays when I first heard him speak of a "hadith" (the words of Muhammad, as recorded by Muslim sages) where Allah

115

says, "I cannot be contained within the Earth or the heavens, but I can be contained within the loving heart of my servant."

Now it made sense! For whatever reason, my mind had heard "fist," where "open hand" might have been more appropriate. The entirety of the universe would not fill the hand of God. And yet, the entirety of God would not fill the hand of the universe. Now I understood and interpreted "Your universe fills not my fist ... nor I it" to mean that while the entirety of the universe would not fill the hand of God, the entirety of God wouldn't completely fill the hand of a single loving human. What, then, to make of the nature of God? It was then that I came to understand God as Cosmic Conscience. The entirety of Cosmic Conscience cannot be contained by even the vastness of our universe. And yet, if we will listen, we can hold Cosmic Conscience in our hands, or, as the hadith so appropriately put it, in our hearts.

Cosmic Conscience can be held in our hands and hearts, but it cannot be bound by them. Cosmic Conscience fills the universe. Cosmic Conscience can and will speak to Jew, Christian, Muslim, Buddhist, Baha'i, Humanist, Sikh, and every and all who live. Cosmic Conscience cannot be bound, boxed or claimed by a single entity but can be heard by every entity. All this made sense.

Now, what to make of, "That which breathes has a soul." Really? Elephants? Ants? Dogs? Fish? "That which breathes has a soul"? After pondering that one for a while, it too made sense to me in that our souls are the repository, if you will, of love and conscience. Anyone who knows animals knows that they show love to their children; except, of course, we call their children offspring, and we often write off the love they show as instinct.

Still, once I got past that, I realized why Cosmic Conscience might think of humans as Children of Conscience or, if you will, Children of God. We humans have a brain, if we choose to use it, and we have opposable thumbs that allow us to build. Even more important, humans can develop complex language to express themselves. We thus have an ability that other animals do not. We can give voice to the call of conscience. In this way, humans, more than any other animal, or at least any animal known to me, have an enormous capacity both to embrace conscience and express love. To be sure, we don't always make good use of that capacity, but we have it. In that way, we can indeed become special to God—if we will make the effort to listen to the call of conscience and allow ourselves to become its vessel.

This brought me to something in the revelations that I confess made me uncomfortable, something that up to now I've carefully avoided. It's the use of the word "creation." "Creation" kept coming up the in the revelations. Why? Cosmic Conscience certainly couldn't create the heaven and the Earth. On the other hand, it occurred to me that the continual call to conscience, to love one another, to act with justice and in community, might be seen as God working within us, creating within us. "Create in me a clean heart, O God." Psalm 51:12.

My interpretation is that I heard "creation" in part at least because that's the word I commonly use when referring to the Earth. "All of creation" is how I tend to refer to everything on the planet. It's a figure of speech and not a way of saying I believe God physically created Earth and life. As best as I understand current science, life on Earth evolved over millions of years rather than being created in six days. With this understanding of what the word *creation* meant to me and how I use it, I have interpreted "my creation" as I have. That said, the word is there. I had and have no desire to try to "edit" what I heard (the one exception being substituting "magic" for "mysticism," as explained earlier, and in detail in *One Family: Indivisible*). So, the word creation is there. I can appreciate and respect that others might interpret it differently than I. Still, thinking about it helped me to understand more clearly that culture shapes our vocabulary.

For me, this helped to answer some nagging questions. Cosmic Conscience called to the ancients, and they interpreted that call as their culture instructed them. Cosmic Conscience could call to Moses and say that he must go back to Egypt and work to free his people. Cosmic

Conscience could call to Abraham, to Jesus, to Muhammad, to the Buddha, to Bahaullah, and to so many, many others throughout time—people recorded by history and not. Good grief! Cosmic Conscience could call even to me about being both unbound by the universe and being able to be held in our hand. This was clearly not a new call, as shown by the same call, shared with Islam, though interpreted differently with the heart and not the hand as the vehicle for holding the call of the divine.

If God is the call of Conscience and not some entity that cancels the laws of physics at will (aka "miracles"), then even so it makes sense that ancients might interpret the call of Conscience in terms of miracles. Then, as humanity learned more about the world, gaining at last a telescope and began to understand physics and our place in the universe, it also makes sense that these so-called "miracles" would seem to disappear. If you will, God hasn't changed, but we have, and, unless we blot ourselves into oblivion, we will continue to change.

For me, then, God did not deliver Daniel from the lion's den and the Hebrew Children from Egypt, and then get bored with it all and stop with the miracle-making. Conscience called to Daniel and to Moses, and they answered that call. I believe the call of Conscience reached Harriet Tubman, and she helped create the Underground Railroad. The call of Cosmic Conscience remains. The question is always, will we listen? And more than listening, will we then act on that call?

That left for me one last large and baffling conundrum. If God is Cosmic Conscience and not a miracle-maker, what, then, do we do about prayer? All of our spiritual traditions have one form of prayer or another. What's the point? I believe the point is huge.

First, while I cannot possibly understand the whole of it, I believe that each and all of us put energy out in the world and the universe. I believe praying for a positive outcome puts positive energy into the air. So, I do believe that praying for something positive helps. I also believe that while Cosmic Conscience does *not* decide to answer some prayers

("Please save my sick child." "Okay."), while denying others ("Please save my sick child." "Nah."), our adding positive energy into the world can indeed help to bring comfort.

I believe that a second important reason for prayer takes us back to the previous section. Prayer reminds us that we are *not* all powerful. Prayer reminds us that there are things quite beyond our best efforts. Prayer is, then, an important reminder to us to be humble, and we arrogant humans need that reminder frequently! We're human. While there is much we can do, there is much more that we cannot.

I believe that prayer can also open us to Cosmic Conscience. If our prayer is indeed humble, I believe we are opening ourselves to God. For me, then, "right relationship" with God is a right relationship with the call of Conscience.

CHAPTER SEVENTEEN

In this chapter, I want to deal with three revelations that were, for me, deeply personal and important. I was born just a few years after the Shoah (many still say Holocaust) and was acutely aware of Hitler's attempt to exterminate all of Jewish heritage. I was also aware of the Pope's "Concordat" with Hitler that helped to legitimize both Hitler and Nazi Germany.

I was aware as well of Christian ministers who called Jews "Christ-killers" and consigned (in the name of their God of love) anyone and everyone to hell who didn't agree with their theological view. One result of this view was my growing up in a Jewish neighborhood, as the White Christian establishment would only allow Blacks and Jews to live in certain restricted areas. Last, "God, the father" and "Jesus, the son" struck me as yet another disquieting example of patriarchy rearing its ugly head. So, as a youth I had a chip on my shoulder regarding Christianity. It was a huge chip.

Then, life intervened. I ended up going to a wonderful liberal arts college that had been mostly Protestant Christian. Indeed, I was a part of their liberalizing policy of consciously admitting some Blacks and Jews. At that school, Occidental College, I met some wonderful people who were Christian. It quickly became clear that Christians and Jews had something very specific in common. Just like Jews, there were some Christians you could trust with your life and others you wouldn't want to turn your back on for three seconds. A person saying, "I'm Christian" told me nothing about what kind of person they were. For my young mind, this was indeed a revelation.

After college, my first job as a choir director was at a Methodist Church, where the minister was a wonderful human being whose commitment to justice for all his brothers and sisters caused him to risk his life marching for racial justice in the South at a time when so doing could get you killed. I became friends with another Methodist minister who also became a mentor. He too had spent much of his life committed to love and justice for all his brothers and sisters. I met, fell in love with, and would have married, had she not been killed in a traffic accident, a Catholic woman who was not only justice and compassion oriented, but also introduced me to her priest. He didn't simply accept and respect me as her Jewish future husband. He was also deeply committed to love and justice around the world. So much for that chip. It left my shoulder forever. I had learned to embrace my Christian brothers and sisters who acted in the world with compassion and an abiding love of justice with the same joy as I had embracing my fellow Jewish brothers and sisters who acted similarly in the world.

Still, how to deal with Jesus on a personal level remained a true conundrum. The conundrum remained unresolved until the revelations made things clear to me. What I need to repeat before continuing is that it made things clear to *me*. I can only speak of my own beliefs and how I interpreted what I saw as deeply clarifying revelations.

Jesus was a teacher I sent you. I loved him as a son, but I am God.

As I understood it, which is all I can speak to, this addressed two extremely important yet very different topics.

"Jesus was a teacher I sent you." Okay, then. Jesus was Jewish, and he was a teacher sent into the world by Cosmic Conscience. I felt this meant that I needed to pay much closer attention to what Jesus had taught. I needed to study his words more carefully. And I've done so. While I certainly lay no claim to being a Christian scripture scholar, I have studied and, as the reader may notice, frequently quote from Christian scripture. I feel my life has indeed been enriched by that study.

One quick example comes from my study of Mark 14:22-25 and the paper I wrote about it for my "Christian Scripture" class when I was studying for ministry (see Appendix, but be warned it's a graduate school paper with *lots* of footnotes!). My thoughts came from approaching Jesus' words to his disciples with Jewish, rather than Christian, eyes. Important to the Passover Seder are matzo (unleavened bread) and four ritual cups of wine. In Jesus' time (and still today), matzo was thought of as "the bread of affliction" as well as "the bread of poverty." In Jesus' era, the wine was seen as a cup of joy. Thus, it seemed to me that when Jesus broke the matzo and said, "This is my body," he was reminding his disciples that his life's work was ministry to the afflicted and the poor. When Jesus lifted the cup of wine and said "This is my blood," he was reminding them that as serious as his ministry was, it was done with joy. As I wrote in the paper, this certainly is *not* definitive. Still, it puts communion in a rather different light.

"I loved him as a son, but I am God." This also made a lot of sense. We are all "children" of Cosmic Conscience. As life has taught me, some of us are rather naughty children. Indeed, some of us reject the teachings of conscience and act despicably in the world. But others of us embrace Conscience. Indeed, some of us inhale the teachings of Cosmic Conscience and act in concert with them in the world. Clearly, if Jesus was a teacher sent to us by God, then Jesus was one of those people I should be listening to. This was made even clearer by the next revelation.

Go ye into all the world and preach My gospel to every creature: not Matthew's, not Mark's, Luke's, John's, or Paul's.

Did this mean that the writers of the Gospels were "wrong?" No. Emphatically, no! What I took it to mean is that the disciples interpreted what they saw and heard, as we all do. We may or may not wish to embrace their interpretations and can so choose. What we are called to is to seek truth in the commonality of all spiritual paths and to preach the gospel of love, compassion, and justice coming together in community. This is the "gospel" that flows to Jew, Christian, Buddhist, Muslim, Baha'i, Sikh, and Humanist, as well as people who walk the path of so many other spiritual traditions. I also took this as a reminder to embrace love, compassion, and justice and not to be distracted by who was preaching it.

This was so very helpful to me. It meant I could listen to the words and teachings of Jesus without being disturbed by my outrage over patriarchy. And I could do it without what was for me the idea that Conscience was once and only once and forever manifested in just one human. It meant I could listen to the words of Jesus as I listen to the words of the Buddha, as I listen to the words of Muhammad, and as I listen to the words of Hillel, Micah, and so many others that have so much to teach us if we will open our hearts, our minds, and our ears and actually listen.

Last, there was this.

Jesus did not die for your sins. He died of your sins.

I took this to mean that each of us is responsible for our action and inaction in the world. We must make our own atonement, when needed for our actions and inactions if they proved contrary to the call of Conscience. That Jesus died "for our sins" never made sense to me. How I act and how I treat others is my call, my responsibility. I do not believe I am born a sinner, nor, for that matter, born a saint. I'm born a baby human. How deeply I let the call of Conscience into my life is my decision, and that alone will determine the positivity or negativity of my life's path. My mistakes and misjudgments are mine, and I need to own them. For me, I cannot believe that anyone else's atonement, regardless of how dramatic, can possibly replace my own admission of mistakes and active (not passive) resolve to do and be better in the future. This last revelation seemed to make clear that Jesus had died because too many in power, in Judea and in Rome, didn't want to hear the call of Conscience. This made sense; and they should indeed be held accountable by history.

CHAPTER EIGHTEEN

As our journey together comes to a close, first, I thank all who are still reading! I have shared the word of God as best as my mind could process that word and as best as my mind and heart could interpret it. I am an imperfect human and, like all of humanity, a creature of the era and culture in which I live. That said, I have done my heartfelt and honest best to communicate what was revealed to me.

I believe the call of Cosmic Conscience teaches us that it is not the spiritual tradition or specific religion we practice, it's how we practice that tradition and religion. For me, the question is always and forever how do we *act* in the world? Regardless of our beliefs (or non-beliefs), do we act with love, compassion, and justice in the world, without regard to race, ethnicity, gender, religion, or any other division of our human family? Do we strive to walk humbly with our God, however we may define or experience God (or no God)? Are we able to remember that human history has taught us that there are many ways to respond to Cosmic Conscience? Our cultures and life experiences differ and should be respected.

There is so much hurt in the world. So much hate and pain. Climate change threatens us. Continued war threatens us. Our lack of regard for the human community threatens us. The world that our children and grandchildren will live in, if they are to live, is at stake. May we at last, at long last, answer the call of Conscience and work to heal our world. I would like to close this book with love for my human family by gently paraphrasing the words of Abraham Lincoln.

With malice toward none, with charity for all, with firmness in the right as God gives us to see the right, let us strive on to finish the work we are in, to bind up humanity's wounds.

Appendix A
The Complete Text of the
"Dictation" In Order

Religion is but a language for speaking to Me. Think ye that *arbol* is "better" than *tree*? Was old English a "false language" because you now speak modern English?

You have misconstrued hell and heaven. Those who separate themselves from Me in life will be separated from Me in death. No more. No less.

Go ye into all the world and preach *My* gospel to every creature: not Matthew's, not Mark's, Luke's, John's or Paul's.

I have imbued every religion with truth. You have imbued every religion with magic.

Jesus did not die for your sins. He died of your sins.

Cleanse yourselves. Jesus, Moses, Mohammed, the Buddha: they all can provide you soap, but yours is the responsibility for cleansing yourself.

You cannot value wealth and love Me. You cannot worship power and be welcome in My home.

Lift a hand against another and you lift your hand against Me.

Separate the criminal from you, but lift not your hand against him except to defend yourself. Vengeance is Mine. Protect yourselves from harm, but seek not revenge. If you would love Me, love my creation.

Open your hearts to those in need. Think ye that I cannot see? Think ye a phrase muttered in church or mosque or synagogue can hide from Me the truth of your heart?

Yours is not to judge! Yours is to love and help one another.

You have made my creation a sewer and worshipped wealth. Your greed condemns you.

You cannot live forever, but you can be with Me forever. Time is your measure, not Mine.

The mind is not the soul. Nor is the body. Sometimes, the mind decays or the body writhes with pain before the soul has left it. That is indeed a tragedy. Weep, but do not despair.

Love life. Cherish it. Seek to make life better for all within your ability to do so. But life is only a beginning. You but crawl. Do not despise yourselves for crawling. But never fear or forget that as a loving parent I hope one day to walk with you.

Many have spoken for Me. They were righteous, and they did carry My words. But I am not human, and you are not God. Language can be a barrier between us as well as yourselves that can be all but impossible to breach. Seek truth in the commonality of religions—which are but the languages of speaking to Me. Worship not the grammar.

Think ye I prize green eyes over blue? Brown hair over blond? How can you say I would favor one gender over the other, or hold one race as special unto Me and in the same breath pretend you love Me? To hate My creation is to hate Me. To despise My creation is to despise Me.

My children are My children, and I love them all. How dare you think I would choose between them?

This is My commandment. Seek none harm. Love the diversity of your brothers and sisters.

This above all. For so long as you put yourself before others, so long will you lose yourself and your way and increase the distance between us.

That which breathes has a soul. Think ye you understand the space wherein I live? Your universe fills not my fist...nor I it.

Ye who seek to live forever shall die. Ye who seek to live well shall crumble. Ye who seek to live in harmony with all shall know what it is to be blessed.

You cannot love Me and hate your neighbor.

I speak not to command, but so you may know.

Appendix B
An Afternoon's Dictation
Organized by Topic

Interfaith

Religion is but a language for speaking to Me. Think ye that *arbol* is "better" than *tree*? Was old English a "false language" because you now speak modern English?

Many have spoken for Me. They were righteous, and they did carry My words. But I am not human and you are not God. Language can be a barrier between us as well as yourselves that can be all but impossible to breach. Seek truth in the commonality of religions—which are but the languages of speaking to Me. Worship not the grammar.

Dealing with Death and Dying

You have misconstrued hell and heaven. Those who separate themselves from Me in life will be separated from Me in death. No more. No less.

I have imbued every religion with truth. You have imbued every religion with magic.

Love life. Cherish it. Seek to make life better for all within your ability to do so. But life is only a beginning. You but crawl. Do not despise yourselves for crawling. But never fear or forget that as a loving parent I hope one day to walk with you.

You cannot live forever, but you can be with Me forever. Time is your measure, not Mine.

The mind is not the soul. Nor is the body. Sometimes, the mind decays or the body writhes with pain before the soul has left it. That is indeed a tragedy. Weep, but do not despair.

Ye who seek to live forever shall die. Ye who seek to live well shall crumble. Ye who seek to live in harmony with all shall know what it is to be blessed.

Cleanse yourselves. Jesus, Moses, Mohammed, the Buddha: they all can provide you soap, but yours is the responsibility for cleansing yourself.

Love One Another

You cannot love Me and hate your neighbor.

You cannot value wealth and love Me. You cannot worship power and be welcome in My home.

This is My commandment. Seek none harm. Love the diversity of your brothers and sisters.

I speak not to command but so you may know.

Justice

Yours is not to judge! Yours is to love and help one another.

Separate the criminal from you, but lift not your hand against him except to defend yourself. Vengeance is *Mine*. Protect yourselves from harm, but seek not revenge. If you would love Me, love my creation.

This above all. For so long as you put yourself before others, so long will you lose yourself and your way and increase the distance between us.

Open your hearts to those in need. Think ye that I cannot see? Think ye a phrase muttered in church or mosque or synagogue can hide from Me the truth of your heart?

One Family (Community)

Think ye I prize green eyes over blue? Brown hair over blond? How can you say I would favor one gender over the other, or hold one race as special unto Me and in the same breath pretend you love Me? To hate My creation is to hate Me. To despise My creation is to despise Me.

My children are My children, and I love them all. How dare you think I would choose between them?

You have made my creation a sewer and worshipped wealth. Your greed condemns you.

Lift a hand against another, and you lift your hand against Me.

Spiritual Conundrums

That which breathes has a soul. Think ye you understand the space wherein I live? Your universe fills not my fist...nor I it.

Jesus was a teacher I sent you. I loved him as a son, but I am God.

Go ye into all the world and preach *My* gospel to every creature: not Matthew's, not Mark's, Luke's, John's or Paul's.

Jesus did not die for your sins. He died of your sins.

Appendix C
Shavuot Sermon:
Shavuot, Revelation, and Interfaith

(Pondering and writing this sermon helped to clarify my thoughts about revelation.)

This morning we're going to be pondering two related but different subjects. First, we'll look at, explore, and ponder the Jewish holy day of Shavuot. That will take us to a larger question: what is revelation and how do we deal with it? Our lens will be that of Interfaith.

As most will know, Judaism has been around for well over 3,000 years. What many of us may not be familiar with is that Judaism began as the religion of an agricultural people. Two of the most important agricultural holidays are Sukkot, which celebrates the fall harvest, and Shavuot, which celebrates the end of the spring harvest—or at least it did at first.

Shavuot marks the end of 50 days after celebrating Pesach (or Passover). Those 50 days begin with the first fruits of harvest, the barley, and end with the final harvest, the wheat. The days in between are carefully counted and are known as counting the Omer. As you can imagine, that the spring and fall harvests be bountiful is crucial. Survival depends on it. It was deemed equally crucial to remember to thank God for the fruits of the Earth, for the harvest that sustains us. We humans have a tendency to think rather highly of ourselves. You may have noticed. Humility doesn't seem to come naturally to us. We need to be reminded to be humble—

and we need to be reminded rather often. What does God ask of us, the Prophet Micah muses. Only this: act with justice, love compassion, and walk humbly. At Shavuot, we are commanded not simply to harvest our crops, but to take a portion of them to the Temple as an offering of thanks and humility to that which is greater than ourselves. We are tied to the Earth and need to be reminded of that. This year, this Shavuot, as Climate Change is changing the harvests all over the world, it is a good time to remember just how tied to the Earth we arrogant humans are. So, it is good to pause, to remember, and give thanks.

That is the essence, the important, indeed crucial essence, of how Shavuot began, and it would be a good idea to cleave to it today. But, you may ask, what about the first five books of Hebrew scripture, often called the "Five Books of Moses," and even more often called Torah? Isn't Shavuot a celebration of Moses' receipt of the Torah from the hand of God? Isn't Shavuot a celebration of the great revelation that is at the very heart of Judaism? Torah.

The simple answer is "Yes, absolutely!" The more complex answer is, "Well, yes, now, but it wasn't *always* so." No matter how hard we may try, our spiritual traditions aren't static. Over time, Shavuot evolved from a purely agricultural holy day of gratitude and humility to a day to remember and venerate the gift of Torah, revelation from God to Moses and then from Moses to the Children of Israel.

So, how did that happen? How did the 50 days between the barley and wheat harvests become known as the 50 days between the Exodus and revelation of Torah to Moses atop Mount Sinai? After all, the only mention of Shavuot is in Deuteronomy 16:9 and, in passing, Exodus 34.22. Both times, it concerns the harvest, not revelation of Torah.

The truth is, no one can be sure. Some take it to this very day as an article of faith that Shavuot has always been about the gift of Torah to Moses and through him to the Children of Israel. These days, however, many, if not most, biblical scholars believe that after the destruction of the Temple there was no place to take the offering of our crops as a gift to

God. Perhaps worse, with the Temple gone, what could unite us? What could bring us together? Torah. The Torah was and remains central to Judaism. And Shavuot became the holy day that reminds us not only to be humble but also to remember the laws of God, the Decalogue, the Ten Commandments—as well as Genesis, Exodus, and the rest of Torah. But again, none of us were there. We can guess, we can ponder, we can postulate; but we cannot know.

What we do know is that not only did Shavuot become a holy day to remind us of the revelation of Torah through Moses, but it also became much more. Reading of the Book of Ruth as a part of Shavuot, holding high the importance of commitment to the God of Israel, became crucial. Perhaps even more central, counting Omer, counting the days between Passover and Shavuot, became more than just reciting a prayer every night as the days between the harvests counted down. This time became an opportunity to revisit and build on our humility. This became a time for introspection and meditation. In many ways, it became very much like the month of Ramadan in Islam, though without fasting: a time to reflect on who we are and our relationship with each other and with the holy.

And Shavuot has its parallel in Christianity. Indeed, Shavuot is sometimes referred to, in Judaism, as Pentecost. For me, the parallel is striking.

In Judaism, Pentecost is the 50 days between Passover and Shavuot, a celebration of freedom from slavery and the revelation of Torah to the Children of Israel, who would become the Jewish people.

In Christianity, Pentecost is the 50 days between Easter and the descent of the Holy Spirit upon the Apostles and other followers of Jesus who would become Christians. Indeed, many in Christianity see Pentecost as the birthday of their church.

In Buddhism, Bodhi Day in some traditions and Vesak in others commemorates the enlightenment of the Buddha, the revelation he experienced about life.

We mentioned Ramadan earlier. A crucial part of Ramadan is commemorating the first revelation of the Qur'an to Mohammad. This revelation became the core of what would be called Islam: "submission" to God. Once again, humility.

For me, revelation is about humility. We keep needing revelation because we keep letting our arrogance reign victorious over humility. I believe deeply that each time we experience divine revelation, we are reminded, yet again, that we don't know everything and therefore need guidance. We humans need a lot of guidance. This is why we have Hebrew scripture, Christian scripture, the Qur'an, the Adi Granth, and the many, many other writings that express revelation of the sacred.

Let us, then, leave the specific revelation commemorated by Shavuot, receipt of the gift of Torah, and ponder a bit more the nature of revelation itself.

But first, it seems important to reiterate that I'm offering one person's opinion, indeed one person's belief, but that does not make it fact. It's offered as a starting point for discussion, not an ending point that terminates discussion.

It is at one and the same time rarely acknowledged but also so very common that how we see revelation, how we interpret it, becomes stuck, ossified, very much, as they say, written in stone and, like stone, unchangeable. But shouldn't it be? I mean, revelation! Shouldn't that be written in stone? I don't think so. Let me explain why.

First, just for the moment, take this as revelation. (speaking a long string of incomprehensible words) Everyone get that? No? Hmm.

Perhaps that means that revelation isn't self-explanatory. It has to be in our own language, a language we can understand. And even when it's in our own language, it still has to be something that we can grasp. As one example, imagine if, in fluent Hebrew (or Aramaic), God told Moses the truth that energy equals mass times the speed of light squared. Imagine Moses' reaction. Mass? Light has a speed? Squared? What??!!

This is one essential reason why I continually focus not on the differences of our diverse revelations but on the common actions we are called to—*not* that we always *answer* that call. Moses, Jesus, Muhammed, the Buddha, Bahaullah, and so many others have issued a common call: to love one another, including "the stranger," whoever is deemed "the stranger" this week. To act with justice, in community with one another, and with compassion. The *why* we should do that differs in our diverse scriptures and revelations, but that *this* is how we should treat one another is universal.

I came to this realization from my own experience of revelation. It occurred some 20 years ago and changed my life forever. It put me on the path that I still walk and will walk until the day I die: the path of Interfaith.

Twenty years ago, my life had reached a crisis point. The world made no sense to me. None. And every day, multiple times every day, I spoke out loud or silently from my heart, "God, you're there? Do with me what you will afterward; but I want five minutes, and I want answers!" I did this for months: four, five, six—I'm not sure. Then, I heard that still, small voice of the sacred. "Get a pen," I was told. "Get some paper. Write!" So, I did—some three pages of dictation. No, I won't inflict all of it on you here, but out of the box, this is the very first thing I was told and wrote down (I quote):

"Religion is but a language for speaking to Me. Think ye that *arbol* is "better" than *tree*? Was Old English a "false language" because you now speak modern English?"

Okay. This was a revelation indeed. It opened both my eyes and my heart. "Religion is but a language for speaking to Me." Yes. And no one language is better than another. I may well be more comfortable with the language of my birth, but that doesn't make it better than any other language. What's important is what we say in the language of our choosing for one can write great literature in any language. One can also write pornography in any language. And languages change. Old English did not become a "false language" because it's no longer spoken. One might well ask, why was *arbol* used in contrast to *tree*? I believe the answer is straightforward. Spanish is the only language beyond English that I've ever mastered. The example had to be in Spanish, or I wouldn't have understood it. This revelation that religion is a language for speaking to and about the sacred was my door to Interfaith.

A few more examples from the dictation I took:

"Cleanse yourselves. Jesus, Moses, Muhammed, the Buddha: they can all provide you soap, but yours is the responsibility for cleansing yourself." Two things here. First, clearly talking about bathing will not get you clean—literally or spiritually. To cleanse ourselves spiritually, our leaders can provide us soap, but it is our job to cleanse ourselves. Okay then, we need to take active responsibility for our lives. Second, and perhaps more important because of how I believe we have misconstrued revelation, why, some may ask, were only Jesus, Moses, Muhammad, and the Buddha mentioned? Why? Because these were the spiritual leaders I knew of. I learned of the Baha'i and Bahaullah several years later, but if I'd heard "Bahaullah" at that time my reaction would have been, "Huh? Who? What?" The same holds true for any number of truly important spiritual leaders that weren't *as yet* in my lexicon. So again, revelation is limited by what we know and can understand.

"Think ye I prize green eyes over blue? Brown hair over blond? How can you say I would favor one gender over the other, or hold one race as special unto Me and in the same breath pretend you love Me?" This one is pretty straightforward.

"Many have spoken for Me. They were righteous, and they did carry My words. But I am not human and you are not God. Language can be a barrier between us as well as yourselves that can be all but impossible to breach. Seek truth in the commonality of religions—which are but the languages of speaking to Me. Worship not the grammar." This revelation guided me to Interfaith as a faith in my soul, heart, and mind.

I share this sampling of the revelation I received for two reasons.

First, once again, I could only receive what I could understand. For me, now, as I look at the diversity of our spiritual traditions and the diversity of revelations that helped to found them, I realize that revelations reflect the culture of those receiving them. Grammar is important. Indeed, grammar forms the glue of every language—verbal and spiritual. But the injunction, "Worship not the grammar," was again leading me to understand that while all of our spiritual paths, our languages for speaking to and about the sacred, need grammar. Jewish? Wear a yarmulke when you pray. Christian (Catholic)? Cross yourself when you pray. Muslim? Face Mecca when you pray. The grammar helps us and gives us direction, but we shouldn't worship it. We shouldn't hold it up as the one right grammar. In English, we say *a beautiful house*. In Spanish, we say, *una casa bonita* (a house beautiful). We need grammar, but one isn't "right" and the other "wrong".

The second reason I wanted to share my revelations was … look at me. I'm nothing special. I'm no one special. So, why did I receive the revelation, my "dictation"? I believe it is because I was both desperately asking for answers and was open to hearing not necessarily what I wanted to hear but what God or the Universe was willing to share with me. I believe that each and all of us, if we truly open our hearts, are candidates for revelation.

I would close with this simple but very powerful short sentence from the dictation. "You cannot love Me and hate your neighbor."

Yes, I believe that all revelation, stripped of its cultural grammar, is about love--*not* proclaiming love but acting with love, unmeasured love—not a love for "us" against "them" but love, compassion, and community for all of creation.

Amen.

Appendix D
Exegetical Study of Mark 14:12-25

(This study led to my interpretation of communion.)

Familiarity may or may not breed contempt, but it almost certainly breeds inattention. The story of the Last Supper has been told for 2000 years. We have heard the varying Gospel and Pauline versions of Jesus' invitation to "Take, eat," endlessly repeated. Scholars still write about the Last Supper, but certain elements of it have become so familiar, so repeated, so ingrained, that we haven't seemed to look at them. For example, scholars take the bread and wine that Jesus invokes and ponder about what Jesus meant, but a first question seems to be missed. *Why* would Jesus choose bread and wine as his symbols? This question comes up, of course, only once one realizes how many symbols Jesus had available to him at the Passover Seder.[2]

While we will limit ourselves to looking specifically at Mark, it must be noted that Matthew, Mark, and Luke all make it clear that this was not merely Jesus' Last Supper, but a Passover Service. The Gospel of John disagrees. Some scholars disagree as well. It is important, therefore, to

---

2. I would like to thank Professors Karen Barta and James Eblen for reading this paper and making astute and exceedingly instructive comments on it. That said, any short-comings of the paper are reserved for the author alone.

stipulate that we will *not* attempt to find *the* "correct" interpretation.[3] Rather, it is hoped that by re-examining these few words of scripture we may be able to offer a *possible* interpretation and some implications of that interpretation that are perhaps worth pondering.

With these caveats in mind, what if Matthew, Mark, and Luke are right and the Last Supper is a Passover Seder? What would the Seder look like? Jesus, of course, is Jewish as is everyone else present. So, what is happening at that service? In short, what does a Passover service look like to a Jew of Jesus' era?

The celebration of Passover was ancient even in Jesus' time. "They shall eat the flesh that same night; they shall eat it roasted over the fire, with unleavened bread and with bitter herbs. ... This day shall be to you one of remembrance: you shall celebrate it as a festival to the LORD through the ages; you shall celebrate it as an institution for all time."[4] Whether one counts from the time of Ramses (roughly 1000 years before Jesus), from the return from exile and the building of the second temple (roughly 500 years before Jesus), or possibly as late as Ezra[5] (roughly 400 years before Jesus), the Passover Seder and the symbols that went with it were by Jesus' time deeply ingrained in Jewish sensibility.

What then *were* the symbols of Passover in Jesus time?

Bokser notes (with hearty agreement from a multitude of sources including Scripture) that there were three elements to the Seder.[6] They

3. It should also be emphasized that this is an interpretation of the Last Supper as it is recorded by Mark and not of the Eucharist as it came to be practiced. The two are most assuredly not interchangeable, as Robert Daly notes in "Eucharistic Origins: From the New Testament to the Liturgies of the Golden Age" in Theological Studies 66 (2005), a fascinating article with fascinating arguments well beyond the scope of this paper. One of the arguments requires at least a passing comment. Daly cites a proposition that the Eucharist came first and was only later attached to the Passover Seder in an attempt to "integrate Jesus' movement fully within the liturgical institutions of Judaism." (p. 12). It is an interesting chicken-and-egg question. I am skeptical of Daly's assertion. Montefiore's reasoning (see below), which I do find convincing, makes us ask the question, if the attachment to the Seder came later, who in the Jewish community would be persuaded by such an attempt?

4. Exodus 12:8 & 14 *The Jewish Study Bible: Jewish Publication Society Tanakh Translation* (NY: Oxford University Press, 2004).

5. James Sanders, *Torah and Canon* (Philadelphia: Fortress Press, 1972) pp. 50-53.

6. Baruch Bokser, *The Origins of the Seder: The Passover Rite and Early Rabbinic Judaism* (Berkeley: University of California Press, 1984) p. 41.

were roasted lamb (pesah), bitter herbs (moror), and matzo.[7] This is confirmed by Rabbi Gamaliel, who most likely lived one generation after Jesus: "Whoever does not make mention of these three things on Passover does not discharge his duty, and these are they: the Passover-Offering, Unleavened Bread and Bitter herbs."[8] What ought to leap out is that there is no mention of wine as a symbol. Why?

Bokser suggests that wine was at first a part of this festive service simply because it suggested "joy."[9] Stallings would agree[10] and notes from Psalm 104:15, "Wine causes the heart of men to rejoice." Allegorical interpretations of wine came later. Jeremias looks to the Talmud and 200, 279, and 300 CE as possible dates.[11] Thus, wine in Jesus' time, while appreciated and drunk as part of the Passover Seder, was present as a sign of joy, not as a symbol of the Passover itself. We spend this much time regarding wine as a *non-symbol* for Passover because it brings us to what is now an obvious question: What might Jesus be trying to get across when he turned to the wine and said, "This is my blood"?

Let us first consider the three liturgical symbols of Passover.

The Passover lamb (Pesah or Passover Offering) was the most important. Both Bokser and Stallings reference the Jewish historian Josephus. "Approximately 256,500 lambs were offered on one occasion and were feasted on by over 2,700,200 people in the Holy City, who dined in companies of ten, 20, or more persons."[12] The roasted lamb, ritually slaughtered, was clearly the great sacrifice made at Passover.

The bitter herb (moror) seems to have been represented by different herbs at different times, but there is no disagreement as to its purpose

---

7. There are any number of spellings of matzo (matzah, etc.) all referring to the same unleavened bread.

8. Joseph Stallings, *Rediscovering Passover* (San Jose: Resource Publications, 1988, revised 1995) p. 48.

9. Bokser, op. cit. p. 46.

10. Joseph Stallings, op. cit. p. 156.

11. Joachim Jeremias, *The Eucharistic Words of Jesus* (New York: Charles Scribner's sons, 1966) p. 59.

12. Stallings, op. cit. p. 162; Bokser, op. cit. p.25. Even if Josephus is exaggerating, the numbers are staggering.

and symbolism. Slavery was a bitter experience. Every child of Israel must consider that he (or she) had tasted the bitterness of slavery.

The matzo is more complex. Bokser sees it as bread of redemption because the Children of Israel were redeemed from bondage. Jeremias notes that "In Philo we find no less than four allegorical interpretations."[13] These are that unleavened (unfinished) bread holds the promise of the future; that it is the gift of nature (leavening being thought of as artificial); that it is the bread of affliction (and that great tasks call for great sacrifice); and finally that it is a warning to turn away from arrogance. Stallings goes a bit deeper. He notes as well that matzo is traditionally referred to as "the bread of affliction," but "[i]n Deuteronomy, the Passover matzah is called 'the bread of poverty' or *lechem 'oni*."[14]

The traditional saying at the Seder was, "Behold the bread of affliction… ." However, Stallings, again, believes that while the Aramaic *ha lachmah anya* can be translated "bread of affliction," it is most accurately translated as "bread of poverty."[15]

All this to say that if the Last Supper were indeed a Passover Seder, the table before Jesus would be teeming with symbols of great and traditional importance such that everyone present would grasp.

Examining the Text

While they were eating, he took a loaf of bread, and after blessing it he broke it, gave it to them, and said "Take: this is my body." Then he took a cup and after giving thanks he gave it to them, and all of them drank from it. He said to them, "This is my blood of the covenant, which is poured out for many. Truly I tell you, I will never again drink of the fruit of the vine until that day when I drink it new in the kingdom of God."[16]

---

13. Jermias, op. cit. pages 57-58.

14. Stallings, op. cit. p. 38.

15. Stallings, op. cit. p. 39.

16. NRSV

We note first that Jesus blessed the bread, then broke it. So far, the Passover Seder is wholly unchanged. Then Jesus spoke, saying, "Take: this is my body." What can Jesus have meant? Then, he gave thanks[17] for the wine, and everyone drank. Once again, the Passover Seder is wholly unchanged. Then, Jesus spoke, saying "This is my blood..." What can Jesus have meant? Then, Jesus says he will never again drink of the "fruit of the vine[18] until that day when I drink it new in the kingdom of God."

Matzo is Jesus' body. Wine is his blood. We have become so used to these symbols that we don't ask the crucial question why? Jesus has just told the disciples he will be betrayed (14:17). The disciples are understandably distressed. This is Jesus' last chance to address the disciples as a group, and his platform, according to Mark (Mathew and Luke) is the Passover Seder. The roasted lamb (the Passover Offering) sits on the table. Bitter herbs sit on the table. Jesus ignores both. Why?

The question does not interest Brown. He writes simply that "The Last Supper, narrated very briefly in Mark, provides the context for the first of those predictions (that Judas will betray him); and the idea that Judas will give Jesus over offers a dramatic contrast to Jesus' self-giving in the Eucharistic blessing of the bread and wine as his body and blood."[19] Brown does not reference the Last Supper in Mark again.

Higgins delves a little deeper. He questions whether "my blood *of the covenant*" was originally in Mark. He concludes that, "the true explanation seems to be that the words 'of the covenant' are a later addition to the reported utterance of Jesus intended as an interpretation of it in covenant terms."[20] Higgins also notes that "The Jewish scholar C. G. Montefiore in his commentary on Mark wrote of the difficulty of

---

17. Is this the same as blessing? I think so, as the blessing is a giving of thanks to the Lord. Still, Jesus blesses the bread and gives thanks for the wine. See note 25 below.

18. Which is the liturgical wording used when referring to wine at the Seder or a Sabbath meal.

19. Raymond Brown, *An Introduction to the New Testament* (New York: Doubleday 1996) p. 145.

20. A. J. B. Higgins, *The Lord's Supper in the New Testament* (London: SCM Press Ltd. 1952) p. 32. This interpretation is certainly possible, and it makes sense. While others (see France below) confirm that current scholarship has concluded that the word *new* referring to covenant (which appears in some texts) is certainly an interpolation, they still accept *of the covenant* as a part of Mark. Again, we look at possibilities, not certainties.

believing that 'a Palestinian or Galilean Jew could have suggested that in drinking wine his disciples were even symbolically drinking blood.'"[21] Higgins seems convinced that there are ways to finesse this problem but never is able to get back to the Passover table itself. Higgins also lays out the Passover Seder and the Last Supper in columns and assumes Jesus must have compared himself to the Passover lamb during the several hours of the service that Mark ignores,[22] but he gives no citations. He can't. There are none. Moreover, the argument ignores a problem. If Jesus compared himself to the Passover lamb earlier, why does he refer to the matzo when he says "This is my body"?

The commentaries shine minimal light on this issue. France suggests that "body" refers not to the person of Jesus but his death and prefers the translation, "This is my corpse."[23] Again the question arises: if Jesus wants to refer to a sacrificial symbol of himself, why not choose the lamb?

Edwards notes of "This is my body" that "The Aramaic behind 'body' likely meant 'my person,' 'my whole being,' 'my self,' or perhaps 'being.'" and that likewise the Greek word behind "body" is not *sarx* (flesh), but *sōma* (body or perhaps being).[24] Yet again, no thought appears to be given over why this should be applied to the matzo and not the lamb. Why would Jesus characterize his "being," his "self" as the bread of affliction?[25] Edwards does link another breaking of the bread, the "thanking, breaking, distributing" to the disciples in Mark 8:6 to the "breaking, thanking, and distributing" at the Seder.[26] This is interesting, but one feels compelled to note that the bread broken and distributed in 8:6 was not the bread of affliction (poverty).

21. Higgins, op. cit. p. 30.

22. ibid. pages 45-47.

23. R. T. France, *The Gospel of Mark: A Commentary on the Greek Text* (Grand Rapids: Wm. B. Eerdmans 2002), p. 568, where he approvingly quotes Grundry's work.

24. James Edwards, *The Gospel according to Mark* (Grand Rapids: Wm. B. Eerdmans 2002) p. 425.

25. John 6:25-59 goes in a different direction. Was John trying to explain why Jesus chose the matzo over the lamb? Is this why John separates the Last Supper from the Seder? Intriguing to contemplate, but here we are focusing on Mark.

26. Edwards, op. cit. p. 228 note 37. Thus, Edwards seems to see an equivalence between *bless* and *thank* as Jesus "blesses" the bread in Mark 14 but "gives thanks" in Mark 8:6.

Edwards also talks the foreshadowing of Jesus death being tied to Jesus' use of symbols.[27] That is interesting. But again, if Jesus is searching for a death image, why use the bread of affliction? Why not the lamb? Almost immediately, the Christian community will pick up on the idea of Jesus as the Paschal Lamb. Matzo doesn't fit the image of Jesus as the Paschal Lamb. By referencing the matzo, it seems likely that, as seen by Mark, Jesus meant something by "this is my body" other than or beyond a sacrifice.

Likewise, when Jesus said "This is my blood," he indicated the wine, thus going outside of the traditional Passover symbols and choosing something that in his time simply symbolized joy. Why? What was his intent? It is time to come to grips with the Passover table.

Jesus ignored the bitter herbs and instead chose the joy of wine. He ignored the sacrificed lamb and instead chose the bread of poverty (or affliction). One way of understanding Jesus' possible intent is to come to the conclusion that he was consciously using the deeply personal symbols of the Passover Seder to make a point. If so, what might have been that point?

Brown notes a common theme throughout the Gospel of Mark. Whatever it is that Jesus is trying to teach, the disciples don't understand what he's getting at.[28] The Last Supper may mark Jesus' last opportunity to try to define not only himself but his ministry. We know from the passage that precedes the Last Supper that the disciples were at the very least distressed and probably in despair. Jesus must choose his symbols carefully. If Higgins is right, no Jew of Jesus time is going to suggest "even symbolically, drinking blood." Perhaps not symbolically, but he might allegorically. Indeed, the most important element of understanding the Last Supper in this new way is, of all things, perhaps through word stress. We need to think not of the literalness implied by: "This is my *body*" "This is my *blood*." The literal is out of place in this construct. Rather, we will want to think of Jesus as one last time trying to break through to his

---

27. ibid. pages 422-423.

28. Brown, op. cit. p. 157.

followers regarding what his ministry was about. It wasn't about the body and blood of the man standing before them. It was about the ministry that that man had lived. Jesus needs to take them back to their roots.

"*This* is my body," Jesus tells them. Matzo, the bread of poverty, the bread of affliction, the bread of the marginalized.

"*This* is my blood," Jesus tells them. Wine, the joy of life.

These allegorical symbols of the work and life of Jesus illuminate his ministry to the marginalized, the hungry, the homeless, the rejected. It is not a ministry of gloom, of a sullen, magisterial duty. Rather, it is a ministry of joy. It is a ministry of hope.

It should be restated that this is one of many possible interpretations and is not suggested as definitive. So, if indeed what the Last Supper, as Mark understands it, speaks to us about is not of a literal body and blood but of a ministry to the marginalized, done with joyful acknowledgement of God in our lives, what might that mean to us?

It could be seen as a call to the disciples and to us to live outside ourselves, in community with our fellow humanity. More specifically, it can be a call to attend to the bread of poverty, the bread of affliction.

Grassi writes, "When the pertinent passages in Matthew, Mark, and Luke are assembled and reviewed, there is no question that in these Gospels and in the Acts of the Apostles discipleship is closely connected to sharing food with the hungry."[29] Grassi looks at Jesus as a "radical religious reformer" especially concerned with "the deprived classes of Israel."[30] Certainly, the bread of affliction points us in that direction.

I would only add that we should not neglect the wine. Jesus is telling us this is our joyful duty, not our mournful obligation.

---

29. Joseph Grass, *Broken Bread and Broken Bodies* (Maryknoll: Orbis Books 2004 2nd edition) p. 59.

30. Grassi, op. cit. p. 24.

AN AFTER WORD

The impression should not be left that any of my sources agree with me. Stallings, for example, after citing the Passover symbols, comes to the conclusion that Jesus *did* indeed mean that the matzo was his body,[31] and that "His words must have sounded like a thunderclap through the upper room."[32] Edwards implies that Jesus was indeed asking his followers to, in effect, drink his blood.[33] Bokser believes, "The current state of scholarship tends to argue against the identification of the Last Supper as a Seder."[34] I do not say that they are wrong and I am right. I do suggest that they have overlooked the Passover table, that Mark did not, and that it may be worthwhile to look at Mark's view of the Last Supper in a different light.

---

31. Stallings, op. cit. p. 216.

32. ibid. p. 205.

33. Edwards, op. cit. pages 426-427.

34. Bokser, op. cit. pages 25-26.

Appendix E
Re-Examining the 23rd Psalm

I was working on the last parts of this book when I was awakened in the middle of the night (well, two in the morning) by an inner voice telling me that I'd misunderstood a crucial passage in the 23rd Psalm. The 23rd Psalm? Really?? Good grief! I hadn't thought about the psalm for years, decades. Now here it was. Specifically, I was told that "Surely goodness and mercy shall follow me all the days of my life" was not about me and my receiving goodness and mercy. Rather, if the Lord is truly my shepherd, then I will leave goodness and mercy in my wake, wherever I walk. *That* is what goodness and mercy following me meant. Okay.

This put me on the road to rethinking the entirety of the 23rd Psalm. Those thoughts follow, but first a caution. While this was all quite new to me, that doesn't mean it's new. Others may have come to the same conclusion long before I did. This is simply when I learned it. Also, there are many translations into English, and they differ slightly.

"The Lord is my shepherd." That, I realized, carries far more weight than I first imagined. The Lord is *not* my king, *not* a monarch, nor a dictator. A shepherd doesn't rule the flock but guides it. Some in the flock don't accept the guidance. They stray, and, unlike a king or dictator, a shepherd does not hunt down and kill a stray. Also, as the reader will know, I now look to the Lord as Cosmic Conscience. So, the Lord as shepherd is the call of Cosmic Conscience.

"He maketh me to lie down in green pastures; he leadeth me beside the still waters." Nothing earth-shattering here. By following the guidance of Cosmic Conscience, my soul has both fertile ground and calm. This indeed "restoreth my soul." And I am led on the "straight path" of truth, love, and justice in the name of Cosmic Conscience.

We dealt with fear earlier in the book. That lends understanding to this next crucial passage. "Yea, though I walk through the valley of the shadow of death, I will fear no evil, for Thou art with me." For me this is *not* a belief that evil has been banished from the world nor that evil things may not happen to me over my lifetime. Bad things happen. Horrible things can sometimes happen. What this says is that I need not walk in fear of these bad things!! Be not afraid!

"Thy rod and Thy staff, they comfort me." Two important things here. First, the Lord is my shepherd, not my king. Thus, the rod and staff of Lord are guides to help me live a life of conscience and a help for me to stay on the path of love and compassion. Second, the Lord does not deal in deadly thunderbolts or angry fists. The Lord guides us along the path of our lives with the rod and staff of love and compassion. That is indeed a great comfort.

"Thou preparest a table before me in the presence of mine enemies; Thou has anointed my head with oil; my cup runneth over." The Lord will not smite my enemies. People who may wish to hurt me will not be made to disappear, but even should the time come when I must walk through the valley of the shadow of death, I need not be afraid. Rather, I may continue to lead my life as I feel called. I shall eat, drink, and live as I feel called. I shall stay on the path of conscience, regardless of circumstance, and eat at that table, regardless of what my enemies may be serving.

Now it made total sense. "Surely goodness and mercy shall follow me all the days of my life." As I walk the path of love, compassion, justice and community, embracing the call of Cosmic Conscience, I can be confident that I will leave in my wake goodness and mercy. Regardless of circumstance, even if I need to walk through the valley of the shadow of death, I can be confident that I will leave in my wake goodness and mercy. When my life has ended and my soul leaves both mind and body behind, that soul shall join with Cosmic Conscience and dwell in the house of the Lord forever.

For me, then, the 23rd Psalm is a psalm of reassurance in the call of Cosmic Conscience. It is not a psalm reveling in what I will get. It is a psalm assuring me that in following a life of conscience that my life will have meaning. This is indeed comforting, hugely comforting! Is this the "only" possible interpretation? Of course not. Is it the "one, right" interpretation? Of course not. But, having received my middle-of-the-night revelation, it is how I now see it.

CPSIA information can be obtained
at www.ICGtesting.com
Printed in the USA
BVHW052229110523
664021BV00010B/130